DON'T RUN OUT OF MONEY IN RETIREMENT

DON'T RUN OUT OF MONEY IN RETIREMENT

HOW TO INCREASE INCOME, AVOID TAXES, AND KEEP MORE OF WHAT IS YOURS

ALLEN P. HARRIS, CEPA

Published by Advantage, Charleston, South Carolina.
Member of Advantage Media Group.

ADVANTAGE is a registered trademark, and the Advantage colophon is a trademark of Advantage Media Group, Inc.

Printed in the United States of America.

10 9 8 7 6 5 4 3 2 1

ISBN: 978-1-64225-261-3
LCCN: 2022900554

This publication is designed to provide accurate and authoritative information in regard to the subject matter covered. It is sold with the understanding that the publisher is not engaged in rendering legal, accounting, or other professional services. If legal advice or other expert assistance is required, the services of a competent professional person should be sought.

Advantage Media Group is proud to be a part of the Tree Neutral® program. Tree Neutral offsets the number of trees consumed in the production and printing of this book by taking proactive steps such as planting trees in direct proportion to the number of trees used to print books. To learn more about Tree Neutral, please visit **www.treeneutral.com**.

Advantage Media Group is a publisher of business, self-improvement, and professional development books and online learning. We help entrepreneurs, business leaders, and professionals share their Stories, Passion, and Knowledge to help others Learn & Grow. Do you have a manuscript or book idea that you would like us to consider for publishing? Please visit **advantagefamily.com**.

To my Berkshire Money Management family who inspired this book by passionately living its contents.

CONTENTS

THE CULTURE OF CARING

———— o-o-o-o ————

Times of big trouble can open big opportunities for businesses, and during the coronavirus pandemic, Berkshire Money Management (BMM) was ready for a piece of the action. We weren't looking to make a buck, though. We were looking for opportunities to give some bucks away. We were eager to do what we could to help our community because, in the end, community is everything.

The pandemic will not soon be forgotten. Even if you are opening this book years after the crisis has passed, I am sure you will recall it not so fondly. It will be part of humanity's collective memory. Soon after its onset, I and my colleagues at BMM saw that people and businesses throughout our region were struggling. My firm had the means to do something about it. Though we were weathering the crisis well, we recognized our responsibility to reach out.

No business is an island. It is in the community, and the community is in it. I felt that helping our neighbors was our duty as citizens of the beautiful Berkshires, where I was born and where I expect, one day, to die. It's easy to say you care. We vowed to show it.

Refusing to silently accept the way things were, we stepped forward, encouraging others to do the same.

Learning that healthcare workers were lacking masks, gloves, and gowns, we tracked down and delivered those supplies to any medical facility in need of them—in all, nearly fifty thousand gloves and thirty-five thousand masks. Starting in March 2020 and through much of the year, that was my focus. We also commissioned a local sewing group, the Berkshire Seamsters, to make more than five thousand masks and paid for the labor and materials to make thousands more. To help small local restaurants stay in business, our firm donated $20,000 to keep the chefs working by preparing meals for delivery to the Berkshire Medical Center staff. And we handed out about two hundred backpacks filled with the necessary items for small businesses to re-open (e.g., digital thermometers, face shields, social distancing tape and signs).

As people in our community lost jobs and social pressures worsened, we identified other opportunities. We provided funding to buy hundreds of winter coats, boots, and gloves for people in need and to support the staff and residents of a shelter for victims of domestic violence. As a display of solidarity after the May 25, 2020, murder of George Floyd, our firm participated in the Blackout Tuesday event and blacked out all of our advertising for the entire month of June. As the pandemic continued into 2021, we participated in a drive-by food distribution during the day of service commemorating the Rev. Dr. Martin Luther King Jr. In the summer we helped the community come together with socially distanced workout classes, yoga, and family movie nights.

> **A smart business knows that it must look out for those who sustain it.**

A smart business knows that it must look out for those who sustain it—its customers, its employees, and the next generation, which will become both. That is why we contributed seed money to launch a local scholar program to mentor students interested in careers in science, technology, engineering, and math. Our society will depend on that brain power. Strong communities find ways to develop and keep a talented workforce.

Meanwhile, every member of our staff of about a dozen got a $10,001 bonus (a nod to a business-building company I own called 10,001 Hours) in appreciation of their dedication during those tough pandemic days. I added the caveat that they should spend the money locally, favoring the mom-and-pop shops over the national chains. I wanted our dollars to go to our neighbors for the healing of their small businesses. I wanted to further our purpose of service to the community. This would be in keeping with our culture of caring.

Without a purpose, what is the point of a business? Something beyond making more money needs

> A caring company gains a competitive advantage. Purpose drives profits.

to motivate a thriving operation. The bottom line is only one measure of success. The best businesses are faithful to their reason for being, to the special way they serve others. The nature of their products and services may change over time, but they do not deviate from their founding values. A caring company gains a competitive advantage. Purpose drives profits. Some call it "doing well by doing good."

A company dedicated to a purpose will attract not only loyal customers and clients but also top-quality employees who appreciate the chance to make a difference in the world, which often is cited as the driving desire of the many millennials among us. They will dive into projects with more energy and enthusiasm, building the company's reputation. They will pursue opportunities and welcome feedback, knowing that their labors have meaning. And they will stick around, so long as they feel inspired and valued.

Company leaders can refresh their operations by affirming the corporate purpose that has been there all along. They need to rediscover it, if necessary, and champion it throughout the ranks. The leaders set the standards. Company culture comes from the top, and it starts with treating people right, both in-house and out. Managers who treat employees like cogs in the machinery, replaceable and expendable, can expect uninspired performance at best. Businesses that mistreat their customers and clients can expect to fade into the twilight.

Helping business owners is a significant part of what we do at Berkshire Money Management, as I detailed in my previous book, *Build It, Sell It, Profit*.[1] A thriving community needs a strong business base, and we are privileged to help our neighbors build that strength.

I now write this book to explore the other major focus of our business: preparing families for retirement. Families are the building blocks of our society. A community cannot flourish unless those families are doing well.

---

1   Allen P. Harris, *Build It, Sell It, Profit: Taking Care of Business Today to Get Top Dollar When You Retire* (Charleston, SC: Advantage, 2018).

LET'S GET PERSONAL

"I KNOW WHAT YOU GUYS DO!" a silver-haired gent informed me when I introduced myself to him at a conference. I questioned him with my eyes. "I had a financial advisor myself back in the nineties," he said, before proceeding to tell me plenty about himself and his experiences. "You've got quite a job," he said, clicking his tongue and shaking his head solemnly.

"You don't say!" I replied and meant it. He clearly had no idea what people like me do. This fellow was a successful manager in the field of private equity. He knew his stuff. He was no doubt sharp and well informed about many things—except this. Thirty years ago, the money management industry looked different than it does today.

"I'm sure you're one of the good ones," he said with a smile before turning to mix and mingle. I suppose he meant that as a compliment. I didn't get a chance to explain to him what financial advisors do these days. And I don't know what he meant by "one of the good ones." Let me just say I try to act in a way that would make my mom proud and, I think, keeps us ahead of other firms like ours.

Some folks have no idea how much the financial services industry has evolved through the past generation. Some equate financial advisors of all stripes with stockbrokers. And to some, "stockbroker" brings to mind such dirty dealers as Bernie Madoff or Michael Milken or Ivan Boesky.

Frankly, the sales culture persists. Today, instead of those cold calls from the boiler room, the selling is more subtle, with an arm around the shoulder: *You'll be fine, buddy, just sign here, and how are the kids?* Sure, the financial product might serve you very well. Or not. But the commission certainly serves the agent well.

At Berkshire Money Management, when we try to help our people pay less in taxes and make more money, we are offering client-first advice. We advise; we don't get paid to push product. My colleagues and I are not salespeople. We are beholden only to the families we serve and look out solely for their best interests. That is our ethical and legal obligation.

We are among a new breed of family financial planners and wealth managers who do much more than broker stocks and bonds. Our role in managing investments for our clients is an important one, but it is only part of the equation. So much more is involved in preparing families holistically for a safe retirement.

If you are like many of those who visit our offices for the first time, you are likely in your late fifties or early sixties and starting to think about retiring. Though your investment experience may be limited, you have put together a reasonable retirement fund, perhaps a million dollars. You have worked hard for years, and soon you will be needing that money to be working hard for you. You aren't sure, though. Perhaps something recently has shaken your world. Something is on your mind, and you have some questions.

In the chapters ahead, you will find some answers. You will get a comprehensive picture of how a trusted advisor can make all the difference. I offer this book as a clear and concise resource guide covering the most important facets of retirement planning.

It's Money and So Much More

I have devoted my career to the world of investments and financial planning. Before founding Berkshire Money Management in 2001, I worked at two other financial planning and investment firms during the long 1990s bull market. My first brush with the industry was while I was finishing college. I cold-called companies from a list, trying to get through to the top bosses so the firm could sell them on whatever stock I was assigned to pitch. It was dialing for dollars. I was still a kid, really, and all I knew was that everyone around me played the game that way. From there I worked at a firm where my job was to persuade newsletter subscribers to let us manage their portfolios—better leads, warmer calls.

I chose to go independent just as the bubble was bursting for many internet-based firms, a few months before the 9/11 terrorist attacks. You might say that it was not the best of times. Many investment advisors suggested that their clients hold tight and wait it out, a philosophy that eventually worked, in the long term, as markets recovered to all-time highs. In the short term, however, many investors felt shell-shocked as their portfolios plummeted. BMM's philosophy, then and now, was that it's preferable to stay invested but that sometimes the situation warrants a more defensive approach to preserve portfolios.

That is the essence of our investment philosophy at BMM: We try to help families make money and also try to safeguard it during downturns. It is no secret that the market runs in cycles. During downturns, investors should consider switching to protective mode and then reinvest once the market signals that a steady climb is getting underway. Whether to invest conservatively or aggressively is a matter of when each makes sense based on the preponderance of evidence. At BMM, we don't try to time the fluctuations of a few percentage points up or down. We look for the big waves, not the ripples.

> Today's investors increasingly seek professional guidance as they come to realize how tough it is to beat the markets.

Today's investors increasingly seek professional guidance as they come to realize how tough it is to beat the markets. People who are smart in other walks of life are not necessarily savvy investors. They rarely do as well as the indexes that simply reflect how the market is performing as a whole.

The research firm Dalbar regularly compares how well individual portfolios perform with how well stock market indices perform over a twenty-year period.[2] The do-it-yourself investors fall short. Why? They chase hot tips from a neighbor or a rich uncle or the guru of the day. They jump in and out of investments, buying high and selling low. They squint at a computer screen at all hours, fretting over securities that have slipped. With a click of the mouse, the pain goes away. Another click, and once again they are wishing upon a star.

Human nature, in short, often has led to questionable investment decisions, but with an evolution of awareness, investors have been tapping into the power of common sense. They look for bargains, just as they would at the grocery store. Smart shoppers fill their carts with

---

2   Executive Summary of the 2020 Quantitative Analysis of Investor Behavior report.

the best deals. They know better than to wait till the sale is over and buy when the price is highest. Investors should know better, too, but emotions get in the way. Professional advisors can help them recognize irrational decisions.

The complexity of retirement planning requires more than investment advice.

The complexity of retirement planning requires more than investment advice, however. Today's consumers of financial services need a menu of services to help them answer that one question that is never far from the surface. What they want to know is whether they have reached the point where they can retire comfortably but that requires a close look not just at how much money they have saved but what they intend to do with the rest of their lives. They are asking us to do more than manage money. They are looking at how best to manage the years ahead of them. They want to know whether they will be okay.

So many decisions, big and small: Can we afford that dream vacation? Do we need more health insurance? What happens if we need long-term care? What about our mortgage and our credit card debt? How much can we expect to leave to our kids and grandkids? How can we take less of a tax hit? Should we pay off our debt before retiring? And if the economy crashes again, what then? Will we even have enough for groceries?

Some of those questions involve factors that people can control. We examine the numbers, do some strategic planning, and offer solutions. Some questions, however, neither we nor the client can answer with certainty. Tomorrow isn't promised. A health crisis can come seemingly from nowhere. A loved one could die. The economy has a way of defying the best predictions. You cannot know everything that will come your way, but you can anticipate what might and prepare for it. If you know you've got it covered, you can stop worrying about it.

A recent survey asked American workers what they feared most about their retirement years. Their top two concerns were that they would run out of money and that their health would decline, in that order.[3] That response underscores the desire to live a long, independent life, free of financial worries.

As they envision their retirement, our clients want to build a bigger portfolio so that they can build a bigger life. They want to make more money, but not for its own sake. They see a return on investment not just in dollars but in what those dollars can do.

As the conversation has changed from investment strategies to life strategies, the financial tools have evolved. Perhaps you want to set aside college funds for the grandkids in a way that makes sense. You may be thinking about writing your will or setting up a trust. Taxes might be weighing on your mind—how can you protect your estate? For that matter, you may still be deciding whether your life's work should go to the kids or to charity, or both. That is, if anything is left—you keep wondering if you should do something to prevent medical or long-term care costs from taking it all.

Those are just a few of the concerns you can address with creative financial planning. They all involve money, and they all involve more than money.

---

3   Harriet Edelson, "Half of Americans Fear Running Out of Money in Retirement," AARP, May 21, 2019, www.aarp.org/retirement/planning-for-retirement/info-2019/retirees-fear-losing-money.html.

Broader and Deeper

As you can see, people who call themselves financial advisors are not all the same, though that remains a common perception. There are still plenty of Wall Street–style brokers whose allegiance is to the financial house for which they work. They can sell you only the proprietary products of their employer. An insurance salesperson wants you to purchase a policy or annuity that will deliver a nice commission.

I'm not saying those advisors don't care about their clients. Some of them truly do. No way, though, are all financial advisors the same. Many offer an assortment of financial planning services—but others may just say they do. Just because a website lists services such as "financial planning" or "Social Security optimizing" and other buzzwords that will get search engine results doesn't mean they perform those services or have any particular specialization or prowess in them.

At Berkshire Money Management, we must put our clients' interests ahead of our own. We must recommend only what we determine is best for their situation. To earn our keep, we charge a fee on the assets we manage, so our interests are better aligned: We do better when portfolios do better. We are in this together for the long haul.

As Registered Investment Advisors, our firm is regulated by the Securities and Exchange Commission. By law, RIAs must abide by the fiduciary standard of serving your best interests—the highest standard of care established by law. They must avoid conflicts of interest or, if not possible, mitigate and disclose them to clients and prospects clearly and conspicuously. Their advice must be based on complete, accurate information, and they must monitor the results.

They aren't in the business of selling and forgetting. What they do must make sense for you, not just for them.

At Berkshire Money Management, we provide a suite of services that run broad and deep. We help our clients with financial planning, estate planning, tax management, Social Security and Medicare planning, and more. We help clients develop the income streams they will need to last throughout retirement.

We don't just refer our clients to a Social Security calculator, for example. We work with them on their individual family needs and step them through the pros and cons of when to file. And when the time comes, we get the filing done. For our clients who own businesses, we refer them to 10,001 Hours, which can guide them to their peak performance and value so that they can sell at a premium when they are ready to retire.

Our aim for all our clients is to give them an increased peace of mind, but first they need to feel that they can trust us, and we must earn that trust. We build that trust by getting down to those details that other firms may disregard. We don't just throw a number at them. First we learn about their needs, their wants, and their wishes. We get personal.

CHAPTER 1

MONEY IN MOTION

—————————o-0-0-0-o—————————

SOMETHING ABOUT THE WOMAN'S voice didn't sound right, although it was hard to tell over the phone, with so much noise in the background. Was she in a subway station?

It was the day before Thanksgiving, and she had emailed us a few minutes earlier. She identified herself as one of our clients at Berkshire Money Management and asked would we please electronically transfer some of her money into another account? It was a substantial amount.

She would need to call us to do that, we replied. She complied, but she didn't sound like the client we knew so well. The voice seemed harsher. She provided some personal information for verification, but we could barely hear her over the racket. She said she would call us right back and hung up.

We waited to see if the woman would call us back, as she said she would. She did. She then proceeded to verify everything that we would require, and more, if we had chosen to proceed. She had enough detail to initiate an electronic transfer through a large financial firm.

We immediately called the client's work number, and she answered—with no subway noise in the background. Having talked with her so many times, we recognized the familiar timbre of her voice.

"No! That certainly was not me," she said.

"Well, someone has your information and is trying to get into your accounts," we told her. We then walked her through the steps necessary to immediately protect herself. We learned that her email address and phone number had been cloned.

> A trusting relationship is central to effective financial advising.

Though the impostor was never apprehended, the ploy didn't work because we knew our client well enough to recognize her voice and had implemented call-back identity verification protocols designed to safeguard client assets. We had built a relationship based on trust, and it had saved her from a nightmare. It was one more reason to be thankful that holiday season.

A trusting relationship is central to effective financial advising. It can fend off a world of trouble and open up a world of opportunities. Our relationships with clients generally start when they come to us for help with some pressing issue. Something has happened, or they see it coming, and it will have financial repercussions. It could be something good or something troubling, perhaps both, but it feels urgent. They realize they need to act, but how? They are entering unexplored territory, and they want a partner to walk them through it.

We call this "money in motion," a common term in the financial services world. The concept is simple, really: Money in one place is moving to another place. Your son or daughter is entering college, and the money will be moving from your account to the bursar's office. You're thinking of selling your business, and your share of its value will be moving to a buyer, whether that's a partner, your kids, or an outside party. Maybe you just got a promotion or a great new job and think now's the time for a big purchase—a house, a sports car. Perhaps you have lost your job, and your living expenses are swallowing your savings. You have received an inheritance, and you will be getting a piece of dear Aunt Martha's estate. You are getting married or divorced and find yourself doing multiplication and division problems. Your spouse is seriously ill, and you're sick from worry—will they recover? Will your finances?

The Information Age has changed the timing of a client's first visit to a financial planner. Into the early years of the new millennium, the primary reason people engaged with us at Berkshire Money Management was that retirement already was upon them, and they figured they had better learn a thing or two. Their money was in motion because they were retiring. For years, they saved money. Now, they were spending that money.

Within a decade or two, new clients were coming in earlier, smartphones in hand. Today, our new clients typically engage with us when they are in their late fifties or early sixties. They still are at least several years from retirement age, but they have been doing some research. They want to prepare. Ideally, they should have come in even earlier, but at least now we can get started.

First, we attend to the matter at hand. To the visitor, it feels unique, but generally we have seen it before. We know what has worked for other people and what has not worked, and we can prescribe a solution. Almost invariably, money in some way is in motion, and that is often what compels people to reach out to us for the first time.

Most people are better at reacting than planning. They get busy, and consulting with an advisor seems easy to put off till another day—until something rocks their world and they have a big decision to make. Once we attend to that matter, we can widen the scene. What people need above all is to see how the immediate concern fits into an overall vision of their future. To plan successfully involves an array of considerations.

In the chapters ahead, we will examine the various interlocking pieces of the planning puzzle. Here, let's take a closer look at some of the life circumstances that could put your money in motion.

Leaving Your Job

Retirement brings a host of opportunities to do other things in life, but it also raises financial questions and concerns, both known and unknown.

The most common question is what to do with the company retirement plan, usually a 401(k) or 403(b) or related plan. Do you need to move it? And if so, where? How can you position your money into investments that will grow, create income, or both? The equation might further be complicated by a pension buyout, or a partner buyout, or stock options.

When money is in motion, taxes often become a big consideration. How will you keep them at a minimum? If you just take out a lot of money and spend it, or if you transfer it into the wrong kind of account, you could be hit with a ton of taxes.

You also will need to consider the best way to withdraw your money. Some withdrawals from retirement plans are mandatory, and some are discretionary. And if you make a withdrawal before you are fifty-nine and a half, you are likely to be subjected to an early withdrawal penalty.

The decision-making involved in dealing with a retirement plan can be nuanced, and the cost of mistakes can be significant. It's one of the reasons that people seek professional guidance: They know the conclusion of their job will put that retirement money in motion. They will need it for the rest of their lives, and they want it to end up in the right place at the right time to serve their needs and wants. And that's just the first step. Next, they will need to convert that sum of money into a flow of income, and the big questions there are: *How much will I need?* and *When will I need it?*

Selling Your Business

Business owners have a lot on their minds as they contemplate retirement. Should they sell? To whom? How do they find a buyer and determine a fair price? Should they transition the business to a son or daughter who has shown a keen interest in it, and if so, how is that fair to the other children? If the next generation will assume control of the business, what is the best way to prepare them to do a good job?

Establishing a timeline for the sale or transition well in advance is of utmost importance. Often, business owners underestimate how long that process will take and how much the business is worth. They might have imagined people would line up around the block for the opportunity to purchase what they spent decades building. That doesn't usually happen.

That is why getting an early start is essential when planning for this money in motion. Getting an accurate professional valuation is essential and so is getting it early enough to do something about it. Sometimes it's a matter of cleaning up the property and cleaning up the books so the deal is attractive to potential buyers. Sometimes it's a matter of lowering expectations to line up with reality. Often, it means waiting a few years before putting the money in motion. The best price comes when everything is in order.

And when it is time to structure a deal, business owners are wise to seek professional help with the tax considerations. Sellers often pay too much tax and the wrong kind of tax unnecessarily. A well-planned exit strategy can keep the rates reasonable and the deal fair to both seller and buyer. The seller will want to get a decent price but should also want the business to thrive under the new ownership.

Planning Your Retirement Income

Top of mind for most soon-to-be retirees is how they will replace the income they were getting regularly in paychecks from their employer. Many will be looking at some combination of proceeds from their employee retirement plan, their Social Security benefit, and any other investments that can contribute to the cash flow. Getting that all into place means putting money in motion.

Social Security concerns are among the more common questions we hear. Dealing with the bureaucracy and filling out the forms can feel burdensome to anyone doing this for the first time, and since people generally retire only once, it's the first time for all. Or maybe it's time to file for Medicare. You have to pay for that, so some of your income is going to move toward those payments.

A lot of people think that the best idea is to wait as long as you can before collecting Social Security payments. Taking your benefit early may reduce the check size, but you will receive those checks for a longer period of time. You need to consider your life expectancy to calculate your break-even age to begin withdrawals. And then you should consider spousal strategies, such as the lower-earning spouse taking benefits earlier if the higher-earning spouse can wait for a larger check.

The bulk of many retirees' income is the cash flow generated from an investment portfolio that was built up over years in a company retirement plan. Even if the portfolio starts with enough to theoretically generate enough income to support a standard of living, the portfolio is subject to what is known as a "sequence of return risk," which is the risk that the market—and your portfolio—will crash the day after you retire, which could compromise your retirement hopes.

Receiving an Inheritance

An inheritance from a loved one is more emotional than a standard windfall because there is a person's memory and legacy behind it. Emotions run high. Infighting among heirs is not uncommon. Some families find it helpful to engage a financial coach to facilitate family meetings to set parameters and sort out differences.

You may feel confident about what to do with the inheritance, but a second opinion from an experienced financial advisor is still worth exploring. Friends and relatives likely will have plenty of ideas for how you should spend, invest, or lend the bequest, and it can be hard to say no. It's best to take time with such decisions. You may regret quick decisions made emotionally.

Your loved one would want you to enjoy the bequest but also would want you to make good decisions. Consider these categories for using the money:

- Safety (medical expenses, insurance, home repair, personal transportation, etc.)

- Fun (vacations, dinners, etc.)

- Future (investing)

- Cushion (managed cash for true emergencies)

Many of our clients also add a fifth category, charity. For each of these, you should examine both the tax and the growth considerations. And you should prioritize your financial goals, not simply place equal amounts into each category.

In our experience, even those with significant assets struggle when they receive money or property all at once, as opposed to earning it slowly over a period of time. So it's important that you deal with the human side as well as the logistical side of managing your inheritance.

Going through a Divorce

Most people rely on a lawyer, and sometimes an accountant, to plan on who will get which assets and which liabilities after a divorce. But once that transaction is done, most of those professionals do not have the experience required to plan for lifelong needs. It's best to have a financial advisor involved from the start.

The financial advisor is part of the divorce team. The advisor has a better handle on the best way to navigate pension and retirement plan issues, calculate whether the client can afford the matrimonial home, consider the effects of dividing property, determine how much risk the client can (or should) take in their investments, and do the math on children's education costs.

There will be new incomes, new expenses, and a new mix of assets that will alter projected returns on investments. Those new assumptions will change over time and should be monitored and refined. That's true when you are married, too, but after a divorce, those changes can be bigger, and have a greater impact, than one might expect.

Planning College Expenses

Another of the money in motion situations is when parents are trying to position themselves to qualify for student aid to send a child to college. They want to know how they might reallocate income or assets to increase the amount of aid available to their family.

The Free Application for Federal Student Aid (FAFSA) and the College Scholarship Service (CSS) Profile are based on tax returns before a student's junior year, so some families can reallocate income or assets that might otherwise be on the tax return. For business owners, an efficient strategy could be to invest more in the business now and as a result accept a temporary reduction of income. In the long term, the business will benefit from better growth. In the short term, the lower income will mean lower tuition payments. Other strategies could include maximizing taxable investment contributions and accelerating other payments.

Parents often want to get an early start in setting aside money to pay for those college expenses. They want to know the most sensible way to do so. Grandparents and other loved ones have the same question: How can this be done in combination with student aid, while keeping taxes in mind, to help the children the most? How can they be sure the money will be used as intended?

A variety of financial instruments are available for that purpose, and the best strategy will depend on the family situation. One aspect of the decision is who will control the fund—the parents or grandparents, or the student? If an account is simply opened in the child's name, that child could spend it as they please upon becoming an adult. Some young people can handle that responsibility. Others cannot.

Tailored Solutions

Those examples of money in motion often correlate with retirement. Younger people, of course, also have times of transition that involve major financial decisions: getting married, having a baby, the child leaving the nest, or a parent moving into the house or into an extended care facility. Buying a house and other property also puts money in motion, as does the decision to sell that property.

Starting a business also is bound to raise many questions. If a young entrepreneur fails to ask those questions and address them effectively, the consequence could be disappointment at retirement time. This is why Berkshire Money Management enjoys working with business owners. They understand that they should get an early start on doing it right.

Whenever money is on the move, people wonder what to do. Seldom is there a simple answer. Family and business life can get complicated, and the solutions must be tailored to meet a variety of complex situations.

A lot of our clientele are women who are heads of household. Some have never married; others are widowed or divorced. Typically, though, we are working with married couples, and we find that it is the husband who calls to make an appointment. He'll be retiring soon, he says, and wants to talk over some things that have been on his mind. "Just want to make sure we've got our ducks in a row," he says.

We schedule a time when he can come in. "Great, and I'll bring my stuff; it's all organized," he says and gets ready to hang up.

"Wait, does that time work for your wife's schedule too?" we ask.

"My wife? Well, no. I mean, she won't be coming in."

And that leads us to the first order of business: For married couples, both spouses need to be involved whenever possible. It's the 2020s. It has long been unacceptable for one partner to dominate the direction of planning. Unfortunately, many men today still feel as if it's their household duty to handle the finances. But handling the finances requires handling life goals—and that's a shared experience.

We have learned from experience that when the wife participates, we discover much more about the family dynamics, which helps us put together a workable financial plan for the couple's retirement years.

Even if the wife doesn't do as much talking or ask as many questions as her husband—that, too, is typical—she often will feel concerns that she needs to express. What if she outlives him by decades? Will she be all right? Will the money last long enough to take care of her as a widow? Even if her husband has reassured her, he hasn't eased her fears by sparing her the details. The unknown is a scary place.

> **As advisors, we need to do plenty of listening before we can suggest the right solutions.**

Our first meeting with prospective clients is mostly conversational. As advisors, we need to do plenty of listening before we can suggest the right solutions. In that first conversation, we get a feel for what the client envisions for the years ahead.

The conversation is casual, but it has elements of *The Dan Sullivan Question*, which is the title of the 2009 book by the renowned business coach: "If we were having this discussion three years from today, and you were looking back over those three years, what has to have happened in your life, both personally and professionally, for you to feel happy with your progress?"[4] The answer to that question reveals what people believe is important. Sometimes they never really have thought it through before.

Another approach to defining dreams and goals is to keep searching for the reasons behind the reasons, as Simon Sinek suggests in his book *Start with Why* (2009).[5] When you ask why enough times, you can drill down to people's deepest needs, desires, and fears. You can uncover their governing values and principles. And why would we want to know that? Because we want to design a financial plan that fits the individual and the family. Why? Because we want them to have a prosperous and fulfilling life. Why? Because it is our mission to help people do well.

It's not as if we put people through an inquiry, though. We're not firing "why, why, why" at them or lecturing on the meaning of true happiness. Mostly we are just trying to get to know each other so we can talk easily about what matters most to them. Once we know what they truly would like to accomplish, or what problem they need to solve, we can begin connecting the dots financially.

We start with wealth preservation—not losing money in investments; not losing money to taxes; not losing money unjustly due to divorce, business dissolvement, or overpaying for healthcare. That also includes making sure your assets aren't unjustly taken (insurable losses, litigants, ex-spouses, identity theft). We track tax rates on capital gains and interest payments to be sure we are buying in and selling from the right accounts. Then we proceed to estate planning. It could mean donating the right assets at the right time.

---

4   Dan Sullivan, *The Dan Sullivan Question* (Toronto, ON: Strategic Coach, 2009).

5   Simon Sinek, *Start with Why: How Great Leaders Inspire Everyone to Take Action* (New York: Penguin Books, 2009).

As money managers, our aim is to help investors keep their money after it is in motion and then grow their portfolio to meet their aspirations. That requires regular consultation and customized care from a team dedicated to your best interests—and that team must be working with a variety of tools and know how to use them effectively. With everyone in the loop, the chances of success are greatly improved.

A Team for Your Dreams

We could see how hundreds of thousands of dollars had been slipping away. My colleague had examined a new client's estate plan and told me he was dumbfounded by what he noticed. The gentleman had a $20 million portfolio, and he had entrusted his family lawyer to watch over his affairs, but the lawyer apparently had not noticed opportunities for big savings. It wasn't that something shady was going on. It was just that not much effective work was happening.

It takes teamwork. Financial planning involves many elements that call for specialized skills, education, and expertise. Your financial planner must build a team that includes the array of specialties needed to serve you well.

That attorney, I'm sure, was no dummy. He no doubt had proved himself time and again, but he was not a specialist in estate management. Our team of planners at Berkshire Money Management are not lawyers. They have not passed the bar, but they have set the bar high for service to our clients. They are well versed in estate management and how it fits into the broader picture of financial planning. They also know when to bring in a deeper level of expertise, such as a qualified estate attorney.

The elements of financial planning—the investments, the tax management, the healthcare considerations, the insurances, the income flow for retirement—all interrelate. They do not stand alone. Your decisions in one area will affect your decisions in others. An estate lawyer or a tax lawyer will be able to zero in on the specifics of their disciplines, but they need the big picture, too. Your financial advisor can help you express your individual circumstances and goals for them so that your overall plan will be more meaningful.

That is why team building is essential to financial planning. Serving you effectively will require a team of specialists. When you need specialized help, your advisor should do more than just refer you to another resource. That's about as useful as the yellow pages. You need a network of experts who communicate with one another and with the advisor who understands your background and goals.

Our approach at Berkshire Money Management is for staff members to put their talents and skills to the best, most effective use. They don't draft legal documents. Their gift is recognizing a client's issues, helping to define goals, and then making sure that a plan is set in place to resolve those issues and implement those goals. They know how the client's decisions fit in with the comprehensive plan. Once a strategy is in place, we can call on our team of experts for specialized assistance if necessary.

If a complicated question arises, we set up a consultation session with the specialist. We are there, too, to ensure that the discussion is pertinent to our client's situation. Generic advice won't do. The advice must be a good fit with the client's financial plan.

Then we provide the follow-through—for example, filing the proper applications at the appropriate time for the right Medicare programs. Sure, the client could figure out how to do that, with so much information available online these days, but most people don't want to bother learning to do something complicated that they will need to do only once.

Think of it this way: Would you want to be the one to fix your car's carburetor? If you have that skill, and you enjoy the challenge, and you like getting greasy, maybe you would. As for me, no. I don't doubt that I could learn the steps, but I will leave that job to a pro. It's not the best and most effective use of my time. It's the best and most effective use of my mechanic's time. He has all the right tools in his box and knows how to use them to do the job swiftly and proficiently.

That's the power of partnership and teamwork. It's efficient and thorough, making the best use of everyone's talents and time. In today's complex world of retirement planning, with so much money in motion, it's not enough that we provide a bigger toolbox for our clients. We make sure those tools are used by the right people for the right job at the right time.

We manage money, and we believe we do it well. We also are in the business of managing dreams. On the cusp of retirement, people worry, understandably, about running out of money. They come to us asking whether they will be okay. We want you to be more than okay. We want your cup to run over. We want you to build the resources to finance your dreams.

CHAPTER 2

FINANCIAL PLANNING 101

"IF YOUR ONLY TOOL IS A HAMMER," the old saying goes, "then every problem looks like a nail." An annuity salesperson may prescribe an annuity to cure what ails you. A banker type may set you up with an irrevocable trust that keeps paying the bank. And a stockbroker may be quick to pitch the investment of the hour. Each has one primary tool and will try to use it, no matter how clumsy or inappropriate for the task at hand.

Some financial advisors today still are the old guard who use the outdated business model of the 1990s. Plenty of younger advisors have been indoctrinated and mentored to take their place. If you go to them with your questions, they may be eager to hammer down their solution to your problems and goals. Their advice tends to be a wham and a bang: *Buy this stock today before you lose out on a great deal! And sell that mutual fund—here's a hot one you need now!*

Most would agree that you'd be better served by an advisor with a bigger toolbox who is willing and able to use what's inside. I have met financial advisors who just go through the motions, if that. For example, some default to telling clients to wait as long as possible before claiming Social Security without considering possibly higher-yielding options. That works for many, but they don't thoroughly check that it's right for the individual. The client complies, figuring that the advisor is a pro and that the pros all would recommend pretty much the same thing. If a client has Medicare questions, some advisors might simply suggest visiting the Medicare website, where the client finds a confusing array of options and costs. When an advisor just copies and pastes some generic online advice, instead of explaining the options and offering guidance, the client figures that's what all firms do.

"Financial planning" means different things to different people; the term does not have an official definition. The words are vague enough that they could describe what a lot of folks do, from the governors of the Federal Reserve to the kid counting coins in a piggy bank. The term does have an official definition from the Certified Financial Planner Board of Standards, a nonprofit that sets and enforces requirements for CFP certification: "Financial planning is a collaborative process," the board states, "that helps maximize a client's potential for meeting life goals through financial advice that integrates relevant elements of the client's personal and financial circumstances."[6] So true. The way I think of it, my job is to keep my clients from overlooking whatever might cause them to run out of money for what they need and want.

Financial planning gets complex, but day by day it can be as simple as answering one-off questions of varying complexity: Should I convert my traditional IRA to a Roth IRA? Should I set up a SEP or a 401(k) to maximize personal contributions to a small business

---

6   CFP Board, "The 7 Step Financial Planning Process," November 21, 2018, www.cfp.net/ethics/compliance-resources/2018/11/focus-on-ethics---the-7-step-financial-planning-process.

retirement plan? Is a reverse mortgage a good option? Does it make sense to sell some investments to pay off my mortgage? How about long-term care insurance? Is there a way to reduce estate taxes for my heirs? How much life insurance do I need? When should I file for Social Security benefits? What's a good place to put my money once I've maximized my 401(k) and IRA contributions? Could I retire earlier if I sell my lake house? Should I start investing more conservatively?

Though those questions can be addressed in the comprehensive financial plan, a prepared advisor will be ready with answers as the questions arise. People come to us for clarity. They bring their unknowns to us, and we offer the solutions that we find to be best for them. We help them to get their best shot at reaching their goals. That is what financial planning is all about. To do the job right, we need plenty of good tools.

Starting Isn't Good Enough

I've seen one-page financial plans and one-hundred-page plans. I have found that the best are neither the simplest nor the most complex. They aren't the ones that are drafted by the professionals with the longest tenure or by the advisors with the most letters after their names. The best plans are the ones that are implemented. An unfulfilled plan is merely a testament to what might have been.

"At any given time," an estate attorney once told me, "I'm dealing with a hundred estate plans that somebody set up, but that was it. They never followed through." They showed some initiative to protect their heirs but didn't finish what they started. The trusts were never funded. They just stuck the documents in a safe, out of sight and out of mind. Nothing was updated. Designated trustees never were notified of what they should do. Healthcare proxies knew nothing of the written wishes.

A document is merely paper until it is put into action. A trust is a great estate planning tool for efficiently directing the flow of money the way you want, but it accomplishes nothing if you just shove it in a drawer without funding it and taking the necessary actions. Sadly, that happens. The hard part is figuring out what you want. That doesn't require a law degree. It does require a great deal of discussion and discernment. That's where we come in. We can moderate a family meeting to make sure the client's wishes are clear.

Failure to implement isn't unique to estate planning. It's prevalent in financial planning as well. Some advisors will deliver a plan with bullet points of steps to take, but the plan has no value if it just gathers dust. That's not necessarily the fault of the client. The advisor might not have offered sufficient direction on when to do what. Or maybe the client knew what to do, but there was no partnership or accountability for the client to take action. At BMM, a client relationship manager helps to ensure that the right actions get taken.

> Developing a quality financial plan is just the beginning. It must lead to implementation.

Developing a quality financial plan is just the beginning. It must lead to implementation. You have probably heard the old saw that starting is the most important step. Don't fool yourself. Starting isn't good enough. Unless a plan is put into action, it serves nobody. It is meaningless.

Step by Step

Think of a financial plan as a process. Your life changes. Your circumstances change. You change. And that's why your plan must be able to change, too. It must be flexible. That's why implementation can be a challenge and why it makes sense to partner with an experienced advisor. People feel more comfortable when they understand how things work. They want to know the steps involved in financial planning. They are okay with letting the financial planner work out the details, but first they want to understand the process.

STEP 1: TALKING IT OUT

"My goal? Hmm, maybe to not run out of money." That's the response that financial planners often get when they ask clients the clichéd question, "What are your goals?" The question is too broad to get people thinking, and they don't contemplate their financial future in those terms. And so they give an answer as vague as the question. They say it half-jokingly, but the other half is fear. They are expressing a true worry that most prospective retirees share, and we get that.

Financial planning isn't just a matter of math. A lot of folks presume I must be good at math because of my profession. Actually, I'm probably average, though I'm a wiz with a calculator. The point is financial planning is much more than the things you can count, the quantitative stuff such as your debts, retirement benefits, and insurance coverage. The qualitative is just as important, perhaps more so—the state of your health, your priorities in life, your expectations, your values.

To see whether you are at risk of running out of money, we take a look at how you might spend that money. We ask about your needs, wants, and wishes. Your needs are the basics—how much you intend to spend for shelter, food, utilities, and other fundamentals. Your wants are the expenses of maintaining your desired standard of living. What will it cost, for example, to travel for four weeks every year? How much will you pay to pursue that hobby that you hope will become a source of income? Do you expect to buy a new car every few years? Do you want a boat or a second home? Then come your wishes. Do you dream of restoring classic cars and adding a fully equipped bay in your garage to do so? Do you hope to buy a country estate where you can grow your own food? You should talk with your advisor about all those variables. As the years pass, your needs, wants, and wishes are bound to change, so keep your advisor updated. A change in one goal may affect the possibility of achieving another goal.

STEP 2: GATHERING THE DATA

After learning about the needs, wants, and wishes, the advisor then collects financial data from the client. The big question, then, is this: Are the client's lifestyle requirements in line with their financial situation? In other words, will enough money be available to pay for it all? Does the client have enough income and savings to get through retirement as envisioned?

STEP 3: ANALYZING AND EVALUATING

With all the relevant information in hand, the advisor can calculate the probability of success, whether it's achieving all the client's needs, or all the needs and wants, or all those wishes, too. The advisor considers the client's current actions, or inactions, that could influence the likelihood of having enough money to get through retirement. Only then will the advisor be able to offer recommendations.

Two people can have the exact same set of needs, wants, and wishes, but one has a $5 million portfolio and the other has half a million. The probability of success is going to be much greater for the person with the larger portfolio. For the other, we need to carefully prioritize and plan. Which of their wants and wishes are most important to them, and which might they give up if need be? Those aren't fun conversations, but it is our job to help our clients face realities.

STEP 4: DEVELOPING AND PRESENTING THE PLAN

In the next step, the advisor explains to the client how those recommendations were determined and how they would help to achieve the client's needs, wants, and wishes. The advisor explains when and how to act on those recommendations and specifies who is responsible for what—the next action by the advisor, the next action by the client, and whether third parties need to get involved.

This can be a time for some tough choices. Focusing on one goal will often affect another. The advisor opens a discussion with the client and encourages couples to have a conversation about their money. If a couple needs to decide whether a want or a wish is really worth what it would cost, the advisor can make that discussion less awkward—sort of playing the role of a marriage counselor. A financial situation, or a lack of communication about it, often is a source of marital stress. The feelings involved can be more important than the numbers.

STEP 5: IMPLEMENTING AND MONITORING

Once those issues are resolved, it's time to implement the plan and monitor it so that the client has the greatest possibility of success, including not running out of money in retirement. During those reviews, the advisor responds to any shifts in the client's life or wishes. A financial plan isn't set in stone. The aim is to adapt to the many uncertainties in life. The markets go up and down, of course. You can be pretty sure taxes will just go up, but by how much and how soon? Dreams change, too. Sometimes they get more ambitious, sometimes they mellow. The client needs a plan that not only stays on track but also provides for continuous improvements. That comes by working with an advisor who can unearth things that might have been overlooked and identify solutions.

Don't think of financial planning as budgeting. Most advisors won't ask you to hand over utility bills and track your spending to the penny. Planning isn't intended to be that precise. It can't be. We don't know the future rates of return or changes in costs of living. We can't predict whether you will have a medical emergency. You may identify a new want or decide an old one doesn't matter as much. Financial planning needs to go with the flow.

The Value of Financial Planning

Many people presume that the measure of an advisor is how well the portfolio performs, partly because that's the only financial planning tool they are familiar with. Certainly the aim is to make money, and if you are lucky, you will make more than the average. Hoping for the best returns, many investors look for an investment professional who can give them an edge. However, the pros often fall short. Dalbar studies have found that active money managers tend to perform poorly compared with the averages.[7]

---

7   Dalbar, "Quantitative Analysis of Investor Behavior," accessed September 6, 2021, https://dalbar.com/ProductsAndServices/QAIB.

Mutual fund managers, all in all, do not differ much from one another in the return they can get from the equity markets, and they tend to do no better than the benchmark that they are aiming to beat. In other words, most do not perform better than the market indexes. Usually, in fact, the benchmark wins. In the ten years ending in June 2020, fewer than a quarter of actively managed funds outperformed their passive index fund counterparts.[8]

You hear plenty about the big winners. They are emblazoned on the covers of financial magazines and enshrined in endless ten-best lists. You don't hear so much about the many, many losers, though— that is, until a few of them become the next year's winners as the financial cycles ensue.

Making money isn't the only way to build a portfolio, however. The other way is not losing money—the principle of a penny saved is a penny earned. Research by Morningstar, Vanguard, and Envestnet concluded that a key value of financial advisors, beyond performance, was their influence on their clients' decisions. The Morningstar report calculated that good financial planning decisions had the potential to increase retirement income by 29 percent.[9] The Vanguard report said the potential net gain could be as high as 3 percent annually.[10] The body of research clearly indicates a significant gain from a well-implemented financial plan.

Many investors don't bother working with an advisor because they have heard that the buy-and-hold strategy of an index fund is

---

8   Ben Johnson, "Busting the Myth That Active Funds Do Better in Bear Markets," Morningstar, August 27, 2020, www.morningstar.com/articles/999669/busting-the-myth-that-active-funds-do-better-in-bear-markets.

9   David Blanchett and Paul Kaplan, "Alpha, Beta, and Now ... Gamma," Morningstar, August 28, 2013, www.morningstar.com/content/dam/marketing/shared/research/foundational/677796-AlphaBetaGamma.pdf.

10 Francis M. Kinniry Jr., Colleen M. Jaconetti, Michael A. DiJoseph, Yan Zilbering, and Donald G. Bennyhoff, "Putting a Value on Your Value: Quantifying Vanguard Advisor's Alpha®," Vanguard, February 2019, https://advisors.vanguard.com/iwe/pdf/ISGQVAA.pdf.

likely to perform better. And they are right. What they don't realize, and what those studies prove, is that it's not just about investing. That's the old 1990s model for advisors. Financial planning today reaches beyond investment selection and strives to help clients communicate better, get in touch with their values, and make the most appropriate decisions. Furthermore, in addition to specific security selection, portfolio protection and value can be enhanced by cost-effective implementation, tax-loss selling, rebalancing, asset location, and withdrawal order.

The return that a portfolio can generate is a tool, but your goal is not to just get a higher rate. Your goal is to be able to do the things you want in retirement without running out of money. To reach that goal, you use a variety of tools for generating income and protecting it. Through financial planning, you can put those tools to work at the right time in the right place.

The Functions of an Effective Advisor

What should an advisor bring to the table for a retiree? Mitch Anthony, who has pioneered the concept of financial life planning, identified six key value propositions that planners can provide. They are education, partnership, objectivity, organization, proactivity, and accountability. I call them EPOOPA. It's not the most elegant of acronyms, I know, but it's also hard to forget. Here is how I see each of those core values in action.

EDUCATION

Let's say we have two clients, Jane and Jim, who each have a $10 million portfolio. Jane keeps telling us she has far more than enough to meet her family's needs, so why not take some risks hoping for a bigger payoff. She worries about missing the opportunity to gain more—some call it FOMO, or the fear of missing out. Jim tells us his family could live very well off just a modest investment return from his $10 million, so why put it at risk? He worries about losing what he has gained.

Jane can't say why she wants to go for the growth. She just does. Jim can't say why he's willing to settle for the status quo. He just is. Neither has any specific reason to be worried about their financial future. They both know how money works and what is at stake, but they are taking opposite approaches to their investments. Each is going with a gut feeling that isn't really based on anything tangible.

This is where a financial planner can play a valuable educational role for you. We explain that investment decisions should be attached to specific goals and accomplishments in life. How much risk is reasonable depends not only on your inclinations but also on your aspirations. You should be cautious about taking excessive risk just because you feel you can, until it's too late to stop. Conversely, even if you don't want to take any risk, you should at least know how much exposure you can take and still be confident that you won't run out of money in retirement.

With that in mind, we can start talking about needs, wants, and wishes. We determine what is meaningful to you. And in our experience, those goals often can be achieved with a lower level of risk than one might think. Our clients can be surprised to learn that. They might fancy themselves by nature as aggressive, moderate, or conservative in their investments, but those are just buzzwords unless there is a reason. Often, they haven't thought of risk in terms of dollars they could lose. "I could accept a twenty percent loss," an investor might say, then have second thoughts after realizing that a 20 percent loss could mean that $2 million is wiped out.

Educated investors don't simply wing it. When deciding how much risk to take, they look first at how that decision could influence their ability to reach their goals. They make smarter decisions when they know what is happening in the markets, for better or worse. When they don't know, they go with their gut—and they put their dreams at stake.

PARTNERSHIP

Which of your advisors do you trust most? A lot of people will say it's their accountant. If you have a tax question, an accountant is right there with an answer. They're smart and know how all the numbers should fit in, and that understandably impresses folks. Sometimes you just need to know something specific so that you can resolve a pressing tax matter. Accountants are good at delivering that information, and when they consistently get it right, you come to trust them.

What accountants do not tend to do, however, is engage in the type of conversations that financial advisors have with their clients. Many accountants strive to be great at paperwork and tax *compliance*; financial advisors try to help by focusing on relationships and tax *planning*. These are longer, deeper talks about family, hopes, and dreams. These are talks about what uplifts them and what worries them. Those are the kinds of conversations that build a deeper trust.

Financial advisors engage in conversations that get to the heart of matters, often more so than the client's other advisors. The dialogue extends beyond mathematics. Money issues stir emotions. Sometimes the advisor functions like a therapist.

That's the kind of communication that comes with partnership. As partners, we are not dealing only with the pressing matters that our clients bring to us. We are going deeper into identifying what they view as genuinely important in life. The urgent issues come and go. If a family has a strong foundation, those issues are easier to address. We partner with our clients to help build that foundation. We help them find a context for their decisions.

OBJECTIVITY

We want our clients to have the broadest range of possible solutions. If they need special services that would send them elsewhere, we advise them to go there. We strive to maintain an objectivity that focuses on whatever is in their best interests.

The objective perspective of an advisor helps clients make better decisions based on facts rather than on emotions. Emotions can get the better of anyone, and they are anathema to investors. The advisor can help the client step back and think twice, shortstopping the instinct to "buy high, sell low" that can destroy a portfolio. Economic cycles are powered, in part, by fear and greed. An advisor's neutral perspective can help investors to resist the impulses that lead to bad decisions.

An advisor's objectivity is valuable not only in investment decisions but also in any decisions that can affect the client's financial well-being. For example, a couple's emotional attachment to the family home in which they raised their children might be getting in the way of the best financial decision, now that they are empty nesters. We don't dismiss emotions, but we do present the black-and-white of the situation. Perhaps a couple feels strongly about planning separately for their wants in life. They need an objective perspective on how a new set of priorities could crowd out other goals.

The advisor strives to provide all relevant information needed for the best decisions. This is a fiduciary relationship in which the advice must be in the client's best interests. Fiduciaries must subordinate their own interests to those of their clients. We are required to inform our clients about anything that could be perceived as a material conflict of interest and openly disclose the matter in an easy-to-understand, conspicuous manner.

ORGANIZATION

Good organization brings order to your financial life. It helps you and your advisor to better monitor your retirement path. All the many factors of your financial plan—investments, insurance, estate documents, taxes, and much more—that must be considered together. Effective organization allows easy and timely access to those elements.

To that end, we collaborate with you to pull together all the information required to see where you stand today. Getting a clear view of that starting point allows us to establish the path of where you want to go. With clarity on where we are now and where we're going, we can get underway with confidence. Organization advances the partnership in many ways. It helps to ensure that you get the best objective advice. It makes it easier to be accountable for implementing the plan.

Even in our digital age, people often take a haphazard approach to organization. Volumes of paper still creep through the mail to end up unopened and unfiled, stuffed into shoeboxes and bags. Even folks who otherwise are computer savvy still often fail to take advantage of the ease with which documents can be downloaded or scanned and shown aggregately and clearly on a helpful, intuitive portal. The proper filing can be virtually automatic, and it takes up just kilobytes of space rather than closet space.

Some say they prefer paper because it's safer, but really? It's far more likely that someone will walk away with your grocery bag of important stuff, or that you will mistake it for trash, than a hacker will somehow gain access to your encrypted and password-protected digital vault.

A greater concern, as I see it, is how to gain access to those digital files if something happens to the owner. If the keeper of the passwords passes away, who will be able to get to the documents? Someone needs the authority to view the information as well as a secure system for managing the passwords. That needs to be set up in advance to avoid a load of frustration that likely would come at the same time a family is grieving.

Business owners need to take a further step toward disaster planning. Even if the owner is dead, the business must go on. This requires more planning than simply sharing passwords. Who gets paid what and when? Who owes what and why? Who besides the owner has check-writing authority? What is the succession plan? Who takes control? In a well-run operation, all that should be clearly established and documented. Sometimes it isn't, or nobody seems to know where those documents have been kept. An emergency is no time to be scrambling around trying to find out.

In a larger sense, an effective planner is helping clients to organize their financial lives, whether by advising on their investment choices or on the management of the household cash flow. They work together on insurance, tax, and estate matters. It's all part of getting the house in order. Good organization promotes success.

PROACTIVITY

Our clients seem to most appreciate our advice on questions they have not yet asked and problems they have not yet identified. It's the depth of our relationship that allows us to anticipate their needs even before they themselves may be aware of them. It's an ability we gain through the conversations and discovery of financial planning.

A client might have mentioned, for example, that they might sell a building. Even before the client comes to us with that decision, we can be ready with details such as tax considerations that might influence how, or whether, to move forward. Or by examining a client's insurance policies, we can point out ways to save on premiums. Clients often are surprised to learn that they are overinsured for the intended purpose, and we understand that purpose because they have shared it with us.

Proactivity is the mark of effective financial planners. They don't wait until the questions come. They actively look for what the client has not yet recognized. It's the planner's job to uncover any problems and be ready with solutions.

> By understanding the client's expectations and goals, both financial and nonfinancial, the planner can put in place the steps toward achieving them.

Effective planners do more than anticipate questions, however. They anticipate major life transitions, such as marriage or retirement, and help clients to prepare for them well in advance. Success requires foresight. By understanding the client's expectations and goals, both financial and nonfinancial, the planner can put in place the steps toward achieving them.

Advisors who are part of a well-run organization that encourages continued education are more likely to take a proactive approach. They have the organization's commitment and full support to build their knowledge and capacity to deal proactively with their clients.

ACCOUNTABILITY

Let me emphasize again: A plan is meaningless unless it is implemented. One can plan all the steps toward lofty goals, but it means nothing unless those steps are taken.

What good is an organized system if nobody looks at it? A proactive approach can find solutions to issues that must be addressed, but if those solutions aren't employed, what was the point?

It's all in the doing. Advice is worthless if it isn't put into action. An effective advisor partners with clients to set priorities and regularly reviews their progress with them, sometimes changing course as information and circumstances change. When necessary, the advisor can hold the client's feet to the fire or even do it for them. That's the value of being accountable. It fosters action.

The obvious example of an advisor holding a client accountable would be reminding a thirty-year-old of a commitment to save regularly into an investment account. Many of our clients are three decades older and already have accumulated their retirement fund, but the principle is the same. For example, we might discover through estate planning that a married couple's heirs would save on taxes if the couple split their assets into two separate trusts. Sure, we could just recommend that they call a lawyer to get that done, and sure, we could ask the client at our next review meeting whether it got done, but we know from experience that clients don't always follow through. So we schedule an introduction to our estate planning team and sit with them through the conversations and the process.

It's our job to hold our clients accountable to the actions they need to take to accomplish their goals. We don't want to see anybody forced by a foundering portfolio to go back to work to make up the difference.

CHAPTER 3

ENOUGH TO SEE YOU THROUGH

———————◦-◦-◦-◦———————

NOT ALL THAT LONG AGO, you might have been surprised to find out that there was a millionaire next door. The word "millionaire" once conjured images of top hats and money bags. Today they wear jeans and T-shirts, and they are everywhere. You well might be one yourself, but does that mean you are set for life? Will you have enough money to see you through in comfort for the rest of your days?

You may have heard of the 4 percent rule, which had become a rule of thumb in retirement planning in the mid-1990s. It was advanced by William Bengen, a California advisor who based the formula on his research of historic market behavior. The rule is that if you spent 4 percent of your portfolio annually, you'd be unlikely to run out of money for thirty years. The portfolio should be diversified and invested relatively with a mix of stocks and bonds.

Now let's look at how those numbers play out if you are retiring with a $1 million portfolio. Each year, you can withdraw $40,000, with an inflation adjustment. Is that the kind of income you were anticipating when you pictured yourself as a millionaire retiree? It amounts to about what you would earn working full-time for a year at $20 an hour. Better than minimum wage, yes, but not by all that much anymore.

The thing about a rule of thumb is that some thumbs point up and some point down. Four percent is too low, some advisors say. Too high, say others. And most warn that the formula, even when it works, isn't right for everyone. You must always consider your own needs and expectations. If you follow the rule blindly, it could leave you with too little or too much. The latter might sound great, but will you look back one day and regret that you lived frugally and scrimped when you might have enjoyed yourself more?

As I write this, it has been more than a quarter century since Bill Bengen begat his oft-cited rule. He says he came up with 4 percent as the safe rate for someone retiring under a worst-case scenario, such as October 1968 at the beginning of a long bear market and years of high inflation. Historically, he said, the average safe withdrawal rate has been about 7 percent, and at times it has been as high as 13 percent. Bengen revised his formula in 2006, raising the rate to 4.5 percent. Now retired himself, he says he started with a 5 percent withdrawal from his own portfolio.[11]

I think he's going the wrong way. To me, 3 percent makes more sense. Let's say your investments are 40 percent stocks and 60 percent bonds. The S&P 500 has averaged a 10 percent return since its inception in the 1920s.[12] But that's only 40 percent of your money. The rest is in bonds, and as I write this, the thirty-year US Treasury rate had passed 2 percent and seemed on its way to 3 percent. That's

---

11   Brett Arends, "Opinion: The Inventor of the '4% Rule' Just Changed It," Mar-
      ketWatch, last updated November 3, 2020, www.marketwatch.com/story/
      the-inventor-of-the-4-rule-just-changed-it-11603380557.

12   J. B. Maverick, "What Is the Average Annual Return for the S&P 500?," Investopedia,
      updated June 1, 2021, www.investopedia.com/ask/answers/042415/what-average-
      annual-return-sp-500.asp.

the rate you can expect on 60 percent of your portfolio. If you have $1 million, that means you pull in $40,000 on your stocks and $12,000 on your bonds, totaling $52,000. That's an overall annual return of 5.2 percent on your portfolio.

Does that mean Bengen is right? Think again. What will inflation do to those projections? If you factor in an inflation rate averaging just 2 percent over the years, that would bring your "safe" withdrawal down to the 3 percent range, or about $30,000 on a million. (Even if the thirty-year Treasury does rise, Bengen's expectation of a 10 percent rise in the stock market could be a bit ambitious.)

I'm not discounting the accomplishment of reaching the millionaire threshold. Most people don't come close to saving that much. I'm just suggesting that you should realistically assess what a million dollars can do for you when invested for a retirement income stream. Most prospective retirees are looking for a quarter century or more of comfortable living ahead of them, but comfort is relative. An annual income stream of $40,000 on top of your Social Security checks might be all you expect and want. It all depends on the standard of living you envision for your retirement. You might not need a million to feel like a million bucks. Or you might need a whole lot more.

Brave New World

Most people, when they retire, are leaving the comfort of familiarity. A structured day. Known expenses. And a regular W2 paycheck that they can count on to cover a range of unplanned-for expenses such as a new roof or college tuition. Even if the retiree is a business owner or a 1099 freelancer, they are probably moving from twenty to thirty years of familiar things and into the brave new world of retirement.

In my talks with soon-to-be retirees, I find they mostly are excited and looking forward to this next stage. But a big piece of them wonders whether they will be able to afford it. They are not sure that they will be able to generate enough income without that paycheck to maintain their accustomed lifestyle.

Generally, they haven't put much thought into the expenses they will face—not because they lack sophistication but rather because they are so unsure about where the money will come from that it's tough to consider where it will go. Nonetheless, they must. They need to work out how to maximize and protect an income for retirement. What's the point of knowing your income level if you don't know how much you will need? You could have far more than enough and still feel worried. Or you could feel an unwarranted confidence due to expenses you haven't considered.

I have had people come to our office with just one question: "Can I retire today?" Literally, today. That was their plan, but they figured they should get an affirmation before giving their two-week notice and walking into the unknown. Some even know full well that they are in pretty good shape but want an affirmation that is more emotional than mathematical.

Either way, to do my job, I need to see how they are planning to pay the bills and what those bills might be. Do they have sufficient income to cover their needs? How about to pay for all their wants and maybe a wish or two?

Money In …

For most retirees, the bulk of what they must replace is the W2 paychecks they received during their working years. Most didn't generate an income from a business, and most weren't freelancers with income reported on a Form 1099, although those are other common pay sources that need to be replaced in the retirement years.

For the majority of people, that replacement income will come primarily from their investment portfolio, and for the last four decades, those investments have increasingly been in an employer's 401(k) or 403(b) retirement plan. The days are long past when families depended primarily on company pensions and their Social Security checks to get them through the retirement years. With the rise of the 401(k) and similar contribution plans since the late 1970s, the responsibility for retirement saving and investing has shifted from the employers to the employees. These plans, in which workers set aside a portion of their paycheck each week to grow free of taxes until retirement, have become one of the most important means of retirement savings for American families.

The 401(k) is a great deal in a lot of ways, particularly since the company often matches a portion of the employee contributions. However, now it is the worker, not the company, who decides how to invest the retirement money—or even to participate in the plan at all. That discretion leaves a lot of room for big mistakes, particularly since most people don't know much about investing. It's not unheard of for inexperienced investors to simply choose the first options on the 401(k) menu, take the advice of a favorite uncle, or mimic the choices of a fellow employee who seems pretty smart. Those are not reliable strategies. Those people could be in a different stage of life

> The days are long past when families depended primarily on company pensions and their Social Security checks to get them through the retirement years.

with different priorities and tolerance for risk. A great choice for Mary could be a bad one for John.

Investors in those tax-preferred contribution accounts also need to be aware that they cannot leave the money parked there forever. You can start withdrawing at age fifty-nine and a half (any earlier incurs a 10 percent penalty), but you must start withdrawing annually when you reach your early seventies. That required minimum distribution, or RMD, increases every year. The penalty for missing that withdrawal is a whopping 50 percent. If you forget and are late taking out your first $15,000, for example, Uncle Sam will lay claim to $7,500, and you still must pay the income tax. I haven't seen any of our clients suffer that misfortune. We carefully track those dates and remind the client if we don't see a withdrawal.

In any investment account, including IRAs or trust funds, to minimize your tax burden, it is essential to select the right investments and avoid ones that are inappropriate for that account. The investments should be available to withdraw in an order that will minimize taxes and maximize income. For example, you should place investments that pay dividends and interest in tax-deferred accounts and investments that may be taxed at a lower capital gains rate in a trust account. Then, of course, you need a plan for which portfolio you will draw from first, and when.

Income strategies must keep the tax brackets in mind. If you have money that you can use as income free of taxes, such as investments in a Roth 401(k), municipal bonds, and certain other financial vehicles like health and educational accounts, you can balance the spending of that money with taxable money so that you stay in as low an income tax bracket as possible. You also can use charitable giving to manage the tax bite, again making sure that the money comes from the right places and goes to the right places for the greatest advantage. The goal is tax efficiency, and people often make grievous mistakes that end up sending a lot of their wealth to Uncle Sam unnecessarily.

If your nest egg is invested in the markets, much will depend on whether the bear or the bull visits in the early years of your retirement. It's called "sequence of return risk." If you are retiring at the dawn of a long and strong market rally, your portfolio could grow much more than you anticipated. But if the markets tank at the same time when you must start withdrawing living expenses from your portfolio, you may never recover those early losses.

Let's say you were on your death bed in 1999 and looking back at your retirement years. *Not bad*, you might think. *I had a pretty good run.* But the Roaring Nineties turned into a whimper not long into the new millennium, as the bubble in technology stocks burst. If your retirement started then, you would have been in for quite a different run.

Social Security benefits still play a major role for many retirees. We hear many questions about whether they should file as soon as they can, at age sixty-two, or wait until they are seventy for a larger benefit. We'll go into detail on Social Security and the Medicare system in the next chapter. And though pensions have been disappearing in the private sector, they still are a significant source of retirement income for many people, including teachers, firefighters, and others who work in the public sector. Sometimes the recipient has the option of receiving the pension as a lump sum.

Those are just some of the major sources of retirement income. Others include rents from real estate, an inheritance, the sale of a business, a reverse mortgage, and a variety of other income streams. Some retirees draw an income stream from annuities, in which an insurance company provides regular payments after you turn over your savings. I'm not a fan of annuities. In short, they are usually expensive, and though you get some guaranteed payments, the annuity company sometimes keeps your money. And sometimes the company will write into the contract that it doesn't have to pay you in times of severe economic stress, which, of course, is when you would need your annuity payments more than ever.

Keep in mind that reducing taxes also has the effect of increasing the available retirement income. People save on taxes by such means as withdrawing judiciously from an IRA and a Roth IRA, through tax-conscious estate planning, by giving strategically to family or charities, by taking advantage of health savings accounts, or by changing residency to a more tax-friendly location. Other ways to reduce expenses include downsizing, selecting Medicare options properly, or managing two years of prior income before enrolling in Medicare.

... Money Out

To calculate how much money you will need in retirement, you first need clarity on where the money will go. You must count the costs. Some expenses are obvious, such as paying off the mortgage. Others will be much the same as before retirement, but some will be unpredictable. Life brings surprises to each of us, and some of them can be quite a blow to the pocketbook. Somebody needs major surgery. You discover that termites have been munching on your floor joists. Maybe it's a one-off thing that won't happen again but then along comes some other spending shock. Whatever makes your expenses bigger will effectively make your portfolio smaller. That is why it is important to plan conservatively and expect the unexpected.

Besides the 4 percent rule, here's another "rule" you might have heard: Your retirement income needs to be only 80 percent of what you earned while working. Some advisors suggest 75 percent, or 85 percent. The axiom ignores the fact that retirees often fill their newfound hours with expensive pursuits. Nonetheless, the presumption is that retirees, on average, will spend less, but says who? Will you? That's what matters. Will you want to retire and enjoy only 80 percent of your standard of living?

Many people travel more, particularly in the first few years of retirement. They finally take up a hobby that they dreamed about for years. They dine out more often. They golf, and not just on weekends. Now that they aren't working, they fill their days with activities, and activities tend to get expensive. Meanwhile, their taxes, insurances, home repairs and maintenance, and utilities aren't likely to be getting any cheaper. As they enter retirement, people often still are thinking of paying college costs for their children or grandchildren at the same time they are looking at the expense of skilled care for their parents.

The reality is that during retirement, you should expect to be spending at least the same amount you were spending previously. In fact, you likely will be spending more than that in the first few years. There's no hard-and-fast rule, but it's not unusual for expenses to rise, say, 5 percent for a retired couple as they take their dream vacation or start that home improvement project they had been putting off. That spending eases off after a few years, and it falls further later on, but you can't blindly apply some percentage to your retirement expectations. If you do, you likely will feel a strain on the budget.

Meanwhile, inflation will continue unabated. In your working years, regular pay raises and promotions kept inflation worries at bay. You probably didn't think about it much. In retirement, it's a clear and present danger that drains the energy from savings. To keep up, retirees need to devise their own pay raises from their investments. Often, they fail to take inflation into account. They focus instead on the lifestyle they can expect from their current cash flow and just generally assume that will continue through the years.

Over the last century, the inflation rate has averaged about 3 percent,[13] steadily eroding purchasing power. Even in the late 1970s and early 1980s, when certificates of deposit offered double-digit rates, they could barely keep up with the double-digit inflation of those days. Wasn't it just yesterday that a fine house cost $100,000 and a $10,000 car was luxurious? What would they cost today? But that was decades ago, you say. Yes, and remember that your retirement could continue for decades, too. If inflation continues at an average of 3 percent, something that cost $100 in 2021 will cost about $250 in thirty years. If you are retiring at age sixty-five with an income stream of, say, $70,000, you will need almost $170,000 for the same purchasing power when you are ninety-five.

A Long Way to Go

As medical advances keep people alive ever longer, they are expecting a lot more from a retirement portfolio. In 2020, the combined life expectancy at birth for men and women in the United States was 77.3, a year and a half less than the 2019 figure due to the coronavirus pandemic.[14] Still, that's nearly two decades longer than it was in the mid-1930s, when the Social Security system came on the scene.

Back then, workers often died before reaching retirement age and never collected a Social Security benefit, and originally a surviving

---

13   US Inflation Calculator, "Historical Inflation Rates: 1914–2021," accessed September 6, 2021, www.usinflationcalculator.com/inflation/historical-inflation-rates.

14   Elizabeth Arias, Betzaida Tejada-Vera, Farida Ahmad, and Kenneth D. Kochanek, "Provisional Life Expectancy Estimates for 2020," *Vital Statistics Rapid Release* 015 (July 2021), www.cdc.gov/nchs/data/vsrr/vsrr015-508.pdf.

spouse got nothing. Today, the system is expected to keep paying benefits month after month, year after year, to retirees who often live into their nineties and beyond as well as to the surviving spouse; meanwhile, fewer young workers are paying into the system. It's not surprising that the public is losing confidence. The system was meant as a short-term safety net for a few and now must generate benefits for decades to many.

Through the years, Congress has patched up Social Security by extending the retirement age and taxing the benefits so the system can keep on doing what it wasn't designed to do. We will be seeing more of those fixes to keep the money flowing. Fear not, today's retirees aren't likely to lose their benefits, but inevitably, future generations of retirees will be depending even more on their own savings and investments to see them through.

Something else will be inevitable as people live longer. They will increasingly deal with health issues. Medicine is extending lives, and helping people stay healthier, but all that comes at quite a cost. According to a Fidelity Investment projection, a typical couple who retired in 2021 may pay, on average, $300,000 out of pocket for healthcare expenses through the years. That estimate, in 2019 dollars, presumes they have Medicare coverage, and it doesn't include the potential cost of long-term care, most dental services, or over-the-counter medications.[15]

Now, that estimate is an average. Depending on your health prospects, you might pay far less or far more than that. To get an idea, you might consider whether the folks in your family, particularly your parents and grandparents, have tended to live long, healthy lives, but you cannot know for sure as you head into retirement what

---

15   Fidelity, "How to Plan for Rising Health Care Costs," Fidelity Viewpoints, August 31, 2021, www.fidelity.com/viewpoints/personal-finance/plan-for-rising-health-care-costs.

you will face. Still, that cost estimate gives you a perspective on what many people pay. How, then, does that affect your million-dollar portfolio? You might suppose that you should diminish your expectations by nearly a third, but what if you sail through retirement in great health, seldom needing so much as an aspirin? What then? Should you raise your expectations a third?

> Only if your advisor gets to know you—the challenges you face, the goals you set—will they be qualified to help you assess how much money you will need in retirement.

I pose these questions to make the point that no rule of thumb, whether it's the 80 percent rule or the 4 percent rule, can adequately answer them. Only if your advisor gets to know you—the challenges you face, the goals you set—will they be qualified to help you assess how much money you will need in retirement.

You should not be playing the averages when deciding how much you can withdraw each year from your portfolio. You're not some average. A rule of thumb doesn't account for how much money you and your family will need to support the retirement you envision, and it cannot foresee major expenses that could come your way. You well might spend as many years in retirement as you did on the job. That's a long way to go, and your savings need to be up to the challenge.

In the Loop

The couple was not hurting for money. Anyone could see that, just looking around their house. The husband was a successful businessman whose company was bringing in $30 million a year in revenue. He bought the house in cash for $2.5 million. His wife had a closet, bigger than most people's bedrooms, that she filled with thousand-dollar shoes. They were enjoying life and giving back to the community.

One day as I was chatting with this gentleman, I mentioned that nearly a third of women with household incomes of $200,000 or more reported they often or at least sometimes felt afraid of losing all their money and becoming homeless. I had come across that information in a survey of 2,213 women in households earning $30,000 or more. Overall, 49 percent of the women said that they harbored that fear.[16]

"Isn't it amazing," I said, "that so many women feel that way even when they have plenty of money coming in?"

His wife overheard our conversation. "Oh my God, that's me!" she said. A flash of fear in her eyes spoke volumes.

He turned to his wife. "Don't worry, you're all set," he told her. He probably felt that he was protecting her from worrying about worldly cares. Instead, she was worrying about the unknown.

Whenever anyone feels left out of the loop, fears creep in. This couple, it seems, had not talked much about the financial provisions that he had put in place for the family. He clearly was a good provider and a responsible planner, but it is not unusual that spouses have not yet discussed the details.

Security doesn't arise from ignorance. For anyone with the capacity to think, not knowing doesn't reassure. It only leaves one feeling tentative, groping for something to hold on to, like walking

---

16   Allianz Life Insurance Company of North America and Allianz Life Insurance Company of New York, "The Allianz Women, Money, and Power® Study: Empowered and Underserved," 2016, www.allianzlife.com/-/media/files/allianz/documents/ent_1462_n.pdf?la=en&hash=DB76F6EE3B711B77523AABC237F9B37F6E8F2F21.

through a dark room. Ignorance leaves one feeling at the mercy of things that go bump in the night.

Fear doesn't necessarily motivate. It often paralyzes. This isn't a marital advice book, so here is the financial advice: You are in danger if you are closing in on retirement and don't have a pretty good idea of where the money will come from, where it will go, and whether it will last for three decades or more. You could make unfortunate decisions that could compromise your security in the years ahead. Don't let it happen. Stay in the loop, develop a thorough financial plan, and step forward confidently into a bright tomorrow.

CHAPTER 4

SMART ABOUT COLLEGE

————————————◦-◦-◦-◦————————————

DEBBIE AND JOE were worried that they hadn't saved enough for their three children to attend college. Their twins, Sam and Annie, were high school seniors looking at schools for the coming fall. Their other child would follow in a few years.

The couple had tucked away about $30,000 for each child in 529 savings plans, but they knew that wouldn't go far. They had assumed their income level was too high to get any financial aid, so how in the world could they swing this?

We looked at their profile. Much of their net worth was in the value of the family home and their retirement savings. We explained that those both were nonreportable under federal student aid rules and would not impact financial aid. In addition, the twins both were straight A students and likely could get some level of merit-based aid, perhaps scholarships.

Annie is happy attending a local community college and possibly transferring to a larger institution. Sam wants to go to a private school. The Ivy League and other highly competitive schools often have less merit aid, but Sam was keeping her options open. Her prospects were good for attending a quality school, getting both financial aid and scholarships, and, with her parents' savings, graduating with only a small amount of debt.

A Plan of Attack

Once, college was a career requirement. Now, many people are finding less expensive pathways to an education, such as going to trade school or finding a mentor. Still, if you have a child considering college, you might well be panicking about the costs.

"College planning" is simply a plan of attack to save for those expenses and reduce them. For some, it begins with the birth of a baby; others figure it out when the child is a senior in high school, which is often too late. Beyond the immediate family, the planning can include grandparents, aunts, uncles, cousins, friends, godparents, etc.

> Education planning is a hot topic in the financial advice industry. However, not all financial advisors dig very deeply into it.

We might hear from parents whose teenager is determined to go to Harvard—and now what? Or from parents who want to start saving for their five-year-old. Or from parents who just got a financial aid letter and are utterly confused. Some want to save to pay the whole bill. Others just hope to make a dent. And for others, a big concern is whether the young person should go to college at all. What if they decide to bail out three and a half years in?

Education planning is a hot topic in the financial advice industry. However, not all financial advisors dig very deeply into it. Often, the conversation amounts to little more than determining whether you have saved enough, and if you haven't, how to save more. For many, though, that isn't an option.

So where can the money come from? Here are a few typical sources:

- The savings and income of parents or other family members

- The savings and income of the student

- Financial aid, including grants, scholarships, and loans

COLLEGE PLANNING: FOUR BIG MISTAKES

Mistake #1: Sacrificing retirement resources to pay for college

Mistake #2: Neglecting to submit the FAFSA financial aid form

Mistake #3: Paying for college out of pocket

Mistake #4: Failing to calculate loan repayments

Parent and Student Contributions

The amount you contribute as parents will vary greatly depending on your situation. You may have been saving all along, but you should not do so to the extent that you put your retirement in jeopardy. You don't need to foot the whole bill. Instead, find the right balance. Determine what is best for all concerned and then start saving to meet that goal.

How much can you anticipate paying out of pocket? The FAFSA, or Free Application for Federal Student Aid, calculates an estimated family contribution, or EFC. That figure depends on many factors—school choice, parents' income, the number of children in school at the same time, and more. The EFC you initially see might be alarming, but if you have taken the time to plan, you won't be writing a check for that amount.[17]

For the 2020–2021 school year, the married parents of a college student (assuming no siblings) can earn $24,200 before a single dollar is counted against potential financial aid. That is known as the "income protection allowance." Therefore, consider strategies to reduce earned income. You might contribute to a 401(k) or similar plan, for example, or to a health savings account. You might invest in a life insurance policy. The EFC formula does not include retirement accounts and life insurance policies.[18]

Some parents help to put their kids through school by borrowing against a life insurance policy. If you have a permanent policy with a cash value, the insurer may let you borrow against that value. You potentially could use the money immediately, free of taxes, with no requirement to pay it back. Always consult with a financial/tax professional about such decisions, however.

If you get a financial aid letter that doesn't suit you, you can formally appeal based either on merit or on need. If you cannot afford the estimated family contribution, you will need to demonstrate circumstances supporting that, such as a change in income, disability, divorce, high medical costs, etc. Or perhaps the student's grades improved from time of application to time of acceptance; if so, you can file a merit-based appeal. You must document the change in grades or test scores.

Depending on the school choice, you may have to file not only the FAFSA but also a CSS (College Scholarships Services) Profile.[19]

---

17 Federal Student Aid, "How Aid Is Calculated," accessed September 6, 2021, https://studentaid.gov/complete-aid-process/how-calculated.

18 Federal Student Aid, "The EFC Formula, 2021–2022," August 2020, https://fsapartners.ed.gov/sites/default/files/attachments/2020-08/2122EFCFormulaGuide.pdf.

19 College Board, "CSS Profile," accessed September 6, 2021, https://professionals.collegeboard.org/pdf/css-financial-aid-profile-overview.pdf.

They are similar, but with some key differences. The FAFSA informs schools of what types and amount of federal loans, grants, scholarships, and other assistance you may be eligible for. The CSS is required by a select number of schools, most private. It analyzes how much nonfederal aid you could receive given your circumstances.

The CSS Profile is more comprehensive than the FAFSA. For example, unlike FAFSA, the CSS considers home equity. Another notable difference applies to divorced parents. FAFSA looks only at the custodial parent finances while CSS also requests information on the noncustodial parent.

---

529 SAVINGS PLAN

A 529 savings plan is a tool used to tuck away college savings in a tax-efficient manner. Contributions to the plan will grow tax deferred, and withdrawals are not taxed as income if they are used for qualified education expenses.

A caveat: If you use $20,000 from Grandma's 529 to fund the first year of college, that may count against you for the following year when it comes to financial aid. That $20,000, coming from a nonparent, is viewed as received income. Withdrawals from a parent-owned 529 do not have that impact. However, the money in the parents' 529 will be counted as their assets in the financial aid formula.

Clearly, there are a lot of nuances here, which is why it's key to consider all sides of the equation. Yes, the 529 plan balance might impact potential aid, but it's still tax-free money, if used correctly, that can cover some or all of the bill.[20]

---

20   Kathryn Flynn, "Does a 529 Plan Affect Financial Aid?" Saving for College, September 9, 2020, www.savingforcollege.com/article/yes-your-529-plan-will-affect-financial-aid.

The student's assets are the next obvious source. Has your daughter or son saved anything toward college expenses, perhaps with a summer job? Are they willing to work at an on-campus job? That might sound like a great idea—or is it?

The FAFSA assesses parent and student assets very differently. Students who are dependents are expected to use up to 20 percent of assets that they own. By contrast, parents are expected to use only up to 5.64 percent of their "unprotected" assets toward college expenses.[21]

Let's say your child has saved $20,000. That diligence could result in a financial aid package being reduced by a fifth, or by $4,000. The easy solution is to move the savings account into the parents' name to be assessed at a fraction of that amount (closer to $1,000, versus $4,000). Or spend it! If you will need school or dorm supplies, a computer or phone, or a car to get around campus, you might make those purchases now to avoid the hit on financial aid.

A Financial Aid Strategy

Financial aid is often a big piece of the pie. Let me first dispel the common myth that high earners won't qualify for financial assistance for their school of choice. They often do, and yet some parents, believing they are out of the running, don't even complete the FAFSA.

Melissa, a divorced mother of three daughters, came to our office to share her worry that soon they all would be in college at the same time. One already was enrolled. "I'll be drowning in the bills!" she said. Melissa had two big factors in her favor, however. One, her daughters all were choosing state schools, and two, she was open-minded about finding solutions and changing course.

---

21   CollegeData.com, "FAFSA Assets," accessed September 6, 2021, www.collegedata.com/resources/pay-your-way/how-student-and-parent-assets-affect-your-financial-aid.

Melissa had taken out private loans at 9 percent interest when her eldest daughter entered college. If instead she had gotten a federal student loan, she could have had a zero interest rate during the COVID-19 emergency relief period.[22] A $15,000 loan balance at 9 percent cost her over $1,000 in interest over one year, just because she chose a personal loan over a federal student loan. She's not to blame. Melissa, like many people, didn't fully understand how the loan programs work.

Such negative experiences often make people wary of taking on any additional debt for higher education.

> To a lot of people, debt is a dirty word, but so much depends on how it is managed.

Paying for college out of pocket, however, can end up being the worst use of your money. To a lot of people, debt is a dirty word, but so much depends on how it is managed. If you have an investment earning 6 percent, for example, you are better off leaving your money there and not using it to pay down a 3 percent auto loan.

There are caveats to nearly every strategy, which is why college planning must be customized. If you get stuck with a 9 percent rate, as Melissa did, then it might make sense to pay off some of the balance in cash or to accelerate the loan payments. With a low interest rate, however, it may be better to keep your cash for emergencies or investments and pay the interest to reap the benefit. In any case, the interest on student loans is tax deductible if you itemize; that perk often is overlooked.

If you *do* conclude that it's in your best interests to pay out of pocket, check with the school to see what types of payment plans are

---

22   Federal Student Aid, "Coronavirus Info for Students, Borrowers, and Parents," accessed September 6, 2021, https://studentaid.gov/announcements-events/coronavirus.

available. For a small fee (or sometimes, none), you can spread out the bill.

Federal versus Private Loans

There are two general categories of loans: federal (government funded) and private (through a lender, such as a financial institution or the school itself). Federal loans tend to have lower interest rates and more flexibility.

The most common federal loans are direct subsidized and unsubsidized. With *subsidized* loans, the government will cover the cost of accrued interest while the student is still in school and for a grace period of up to six months after graduation. *Unsubsidized* loans continue to accrue interest while the student is in school, resulting in a higher outstanding loan balance at graduation.

Some students get into trouble by taking out unsubsidized loans for an undergraduate degree and then immediately begin graduate school. Suddenly, they're responsible for making payments on student loans without having begun their career.[23]

In addition to direct federal loans, Parent PLUS loans can be taken out in the parent's name. If you can receive favorable terms on the loan, this can be a smarter and more feasible way to help finance your child's education.[24]

Private loans, in comparison, often have a variable interest rate, making payments less predictable. Once you have a private loan, you cannot refinance or consolidate to make it federal. You can do the opposite, however. That is why federal loans are typically seen as

---

23   Federal Student Aid, "Federal versus Private Loans," accessed September 6, 2021, https://studentaid.gov/understand-aid/types/loans/federal-vs-private.

24   Federal Student Aid, "Parent PLUS Loans," accessed September 6, 2021, https://studentaid.gov/understand-aid/types/loans/plus/parent.

being more flexible. Nonetheless, more than half of undergraduates borrow privately before exhausting their available federal loans.[25]

An array of options can ease repayment of federal loans. Under current rules, some federal loans can be forgiven for certain periods, or the monthly payments can be adjusted. Income-driven repayment (IDR) plans are available for most federal loans, depending on such factors as income, marital status, amount of student loan debt, and family size. The monthly payment will be recalculated based on these factors and can be payable for up to thirty years.

If you get into an IDR payment plan, you could qualify for Public Service Loan Forgiveness (PSLF) after ten years. You must have direct federal loans, be making IDR payments (on time) for ten years, and work in the government or 501(c)(3) nonprofit sector. That is a huge incentive to get into those fields.[26]

Considering all these sources, you can see how it takes various pieces to assemble the whole. There is much to consider, including the return on investment from the college education. Is the graduate likely to get a well-paying job? And what other expenses will come from choosing one school over another?

So many students eagerly take out loans without considering what the repayment period will look like. You wouldn't buy a $40,000 vehicle without reviewing what the loan payments will be and how long they'll last. Yet you might be more willing to take out $40,000 in student loans without totaling the future payments. If you'll be owing $750 per month but expect to earn $1,500 per month, how will you pay down your debt while maintaining your other expenses?

---

25 Student Loan Hero, "US Student Loan Debt Statistics for 2021," updated January 27, 2021, https://studentloanhero.com/student-loan-debt-statistics.

26 Kitces.com, "Student Loan Planning Using Income-Driven Repayment (IDR) Plans," January 15, 2020, www.kitces.com/blog/income-driven-repayment-plans-idr-student-loan-planning-ibr-paye-repaye.

A Major Investment

College isn't the right choice for everyone. The coronavirus pandemic shook the foundation of how some families think about college. And as costs rise, more students are considering trade or vocational schools, which can be a great option. Trade schools tend to offer degrees in less time, resulting in less student debt. However, with scholarships, grants, loans, and other financial assistance, it still is possible to get a four-year bachelor's degree for less than the cost of a trade school.[27]

The average cost of a four-year private college (a for-profit institution) is $138,192. If you make that a nonprofit, you're looking at closer to $215,796—and that's without graduate school.[28] College is a huge investment, and it should be evaluated carefully.

It may be wise for young people to wait a few years before jumping into college, particularly if they are ambivalent about the experience or have no idea what they wish to study. That delay will give them a chance to better decide on a career course—and to save toward the coming expense. In the meantime, learn all you can about the available resources. School guidance counselors, college financial aid officers, and professional financial planners can offer a trove of good advice.

---

27   Kristin Pilgrim, "Trade School vs. College Degree Salaries: Who Makes More?," College Finance, updated May 29, 2020, https://collegefinance.com/plan/trade-school-vs-college-degree-salaries-who-makes-more.

28   Melanie Hanson, "Average Cost of College [2021]: Yearly Tuition + Expenses," EducationData.org, last updated August 15, 2021, https://educationdata.org/average-cost-of-college.

CHAPTER 5

SOCIAL SECURITY AND MEDICARE

───────○-○-○-○───────

WHEN SUSAN WAS sixty-six years old, it was time to file for Social Security benefits. As a widow, she knew that she would be entitled to survivor benefits. However, those benefits would amount to only half of her deceased husband's benefits. Susan's question: Should she file for her own benefits, which would be considerably more, or should she file for the survivor benefits?

An obvious choice, right? That's how it seems to many people, who go for the bigger bang until they do the math. Susan didn't need the additional payout immediately. She was in good health and had other resources, so she decided to hold off and not collect her own benefits until age seventy. The advantage of waiting is that the monthly payment increases several percent every year until it peaks at seventy.

We did the calculations with Susan. Her monthly survivor benefit starting out would be $1,873. But at age seventy, she could file to collect on her own benefit, and the monthly benefit will have grown to $2,871. Her expected lifetime benefit with this strategy would be $662,337. By contrast, if she were to file on her own benefit, initially her monthly income would be $2,147, about $274 a month higher than the survivor benefit. However, the expected lifetime benefit would be $537,169, dramatically lower by $125,168 than the recommended strategy.

Jim and Cindy, also clients of ours, came to us when their Medicare rates went up (and therefore their Social Security payments went down) after Jim sold his business. That was a one-time event, however, so Jim and Cindy filed an appeal. Medicare premiums are based on income, and the higher your income, the higher your premiums. An exception would be if you have income from a one-time event such as selling a business.

> Social Security and Medicare questions tend to come first among the many concerns that people of retirement age bring to us.

The Social Security Administration at first rejected the appeal but reconsidered when we pursued the matter with the help of our partner who specializes in Social Security issues. Jim and Cindy reported that they were reimbursed for months of overpayments. Cindy's benefit went up about $100, and Bob's went up about $210.

Social Security and Medicare questions tend to come first among the many concerns that people of retirement age bring to us. Most of our clients are not expecting to fund their retirement entirely on Social Security, which typically compensates less than half of preretirement income (as much as 75 percent for very low earners, but only 27 percent for high earners).[29] Nonetheless, the benefit is an

---

29   Social Security Administration, "Retirement Benefits," January 2021, www.ssa.gov/pubs/EN-05-10035.pdf.

important part of the retirement income equation, and the question of whether and when to file for the benefit is an immediate concern to resolve.

Medicare, too, is top of mind. As people retire from the workplace, they are eager to get affordable health coverage in place. That is one incentive for those who wait until their full retirement age, when Medicare kicks in. If they retired early at sixty-two, they would need to pay the full premium for the expensive private insurance that they no longer would get from their employer. Even though Medicare has a cost, it is typically less than private insurance.

If you never have applied for Medicare and Social Security before—and that describes virtually everyone entering retirement— you are at big risk of fumbling the ball. A variety of factors inform when you should apply for Social Security. And trying to figure out Medicare can be maddening as you weigh the costs and benefits of the program's alphabet soup of choices—A, B, C, D, tell me which is best for me.

You can't afford a poor choice. To maximize your benefits and coverage, you need to do it right. You need assistance with those decisions. You won't get the best guidance from a clerk at the Social Security office. The folks who work there don't know you. They might have time to offer you some general guidelines and refer you to online information, but they don't have any idea of your family situation and what you are hoping to accomplish. To make the right call, you should be working with a financial advisor who sees you as more than just another face in the retirement crowd.

In this chapter, we will look closer at Social Security and Medicare and examine some things you should know as a foundation for getting the professional assistance you need.

Social Security Insights

About sixty-five million Americans were getting monthly Social Security benefits in 2020, more than a sixth of the population. Most of them, about forty-nine million, were retirees and their dependents; the rest of the payments were for survivor and disability benefits. The average monthly benefit for retirees was $1,514.

You are entitled to benefits if you paid Social Security taxes for ten years. You will see the tax withholding as FICA on your pay stub, in most cases. That stands for the Federal Insurance Contributions Act, and the withholding includes both Social Security and Medicare.

The Social Security Administration no longer mails out annual statements to let you know your projected benefit at retirement, but those statements still are available online. You can set up an account for yourself at www.ssa.gov/myaccount. You aren't allowed to set up an account on behalf of someone else, but it is easy to do and requires only basic personal information.

The years ahead will see the number of retirees surging as a lot fewer younger workers will be paying into the system to support those benefits. For each beneficiary, 2.8 workers currently are contributing from their paychecks. That support will be dropping rapidly to 2.3 workers by 2035, according to projections. At the same time, the number of people age sixty-five and over will increase from fifty-six million to more than seventy-eight million.[30]

There are four basic types of Social Security payments:

- Retirement benefits: This is the monthly payment to people at least sixty-two years of age who have worked for ten years. The amount is based on preretirement earnings (because

---

30 Social Security Administration, "Fact Sheet: Social Security," accessed September 6, 2021, www.ssa.gov/news/press/factsheets/basicfact-alt.pdf.

those who earned more contributed more into the system) and on the age when the retiree elects to begin receiving benefits. Spouses can be eligible for retirement benefits even if they never paid into the program.

- Disability benefits: This is paid to those who cannot work because of disabilities. As is the case with retirement benefits, the amount depends on various factors, and spouses may be eligible.

- Survivor benefits: If the intended beneficiary passes away, eligible survivors (widows or widowers, divorced spouses, children, and same-sex partners) can receive payments. The amount will depend on factors such as the age at which the person died, how much was paid into the system, and the survivor's age and relationship.

- Supplemental benefits: This is for people with limited income and few resources who were unable to pay sufficiently into the Social Security program.

The big question as people get into their sixties is when they should pull the Social Security switch. You probably have heard the rule of thumb—and, again, rules of thumb are no way to make important decisions on matters that depend so much on individual circumstances.

> The big question as people get into their sixties is when they should pull the Social Security switch.

The standard line is that you should wait as long as you can. The rationale is that you will get more that way because the size of the payments is significantly reduced if you begin receiving benefits at age sixty-two, and the benefit increases each year you wait, peaking at age seventy. In truth, waiting to collect might be wise for some, but it might be wrong for you and your family. You could be sacrificing a significant amount of lifetime payments. The decision is too complex to base upon generalities, yet some advisors may not look closely at the particulars and simply tell clients that they will get more money if they wait. What sounds sensible, however, could be inadvisable. So much depends on circumstances. "More money" could mean a larger monthly benefit, but that doesn't necessarily add up to a greater lifetime sum.

Let's look at some of the facts that you need to consider before deciding when to begin collecting Social Security. Though you can elect to start benefits as early as age sixty-two, the standard benefit is based on your full retirement age. For people born in 1954 or earlier, the full retirement age is sixty-six. For people born in 1960 or later, the full retirement age will be sixty-seven. For each year in between, the age at which you will get a full benefit increases by two months.

How does that translate into the monthly payment you can expect? Let's say you are anticipating a benefit of $1,000 at full retirement age. If you were born in 1954 or earlier, that would be reduced to $750 if you retired at sixty-two. It would increase to $1,320 if you waited to age seventy or later. If you were born in 1960 or later, the early benefit would be $700, and the benefit at seventy or later would be $1,240. A calculator on the Social Security website also can help you determine your full retirement age and how much you will receive whether you retire early or decide to wait.[31]

Of course, don't forget that if you decide to wait, you will collect nothing for several years, and if you die while waiting, you will never collect a cent. Retiring early gives you most of your benefit for several

---

31 Social Security Administration, "Benefit Calculators," accessed September 6, 2021, www.ssa.gov/benefits/calculators.

additional years. You would have to live long into retirement to make up for those missed years of payments. That is money that would have been in your pocket, or money that you could have invested. It might feel right to wait for a bigger check. But the math doesn't care about your feelings.

The decision comes down to which suits you better: to be paid a smaller amount for a longer time, or to be paid a larger amount for a shorter time. Though it sounds straightforward, the answer involves a lot of calculations and a lot of soul-searching. The math alone can be boggling, particularly when you start to add spousal benefits into the equation. For our purposes here, I will focus on one aspect to illustrate why the decision is far from easy.

Should You Wait to Collect?

Now or later? That's the big question for many people of retirement age. Should you begin collecting benefits as soon as possible, at age sixty-two, or is it wiser to wait? And the answer is—it depends. Here are some fundamentals to consider:

YOU MIGHT WANT TO TAKE YOUR BENEFIT EARLIER...	YOU MIGHT WANT TO WAIT TO CLAIM YOUR BENEFIT...
If you no longer are working and need your benefits now.	If you intend to continue working. Until your normal retirement age, your income over a certain level will reduce your benefit.
If your health is poor and your spouse isn't likely to live to average life expectancy.	If you still will be working and earning enough to increase taxes on your benefits.
If you earn less than your spouse and they can wait to file for a higher benefit.	If you earn more than your spouse and want to be sure that they would get the highest possible survivor benefit.

SOURCE: Rob Williams, "When Should You Take Social Security?," Charles Schwab, October 5, 2020, https://client.schwab.com/resource-center/insights/content/when-should-you-take-social-security.

Discussion on when to begin benefits often centers on what is known as the "break-even age." If you live to be older than your break-even age, you presumably can expect to come out ahead in the total Social Security payments you will receive. The calculation of that age depends on the amount of your benefits and a number of assumptions, such as (1) the opportunity cost of forgoing years of checks that you will not be able to invest, (2) the effect of inflation, and (3) your life expectancy.

All are significant influences, but the latter is perhaps the most so. If you believe that you will live longer than the average life expectancy, then it might make sense to wait longer to begin collecting benefits. If you have reason to believe that you won't live to the average, then it could make more sense to begin collecting those checks earlier.

Once you have made it to sixty-five, according to Social Security Administration estimates, your life expectancy is eighty-four if you are a man and eighty-six and a half if you are a woman. Married people tend to live even longer, with a chance that one spouse or the other will live to age ninety.

If you are married, there are strategies to maximize the benefits that you will receive. The amount of payments to a surviving, lower-earning spouse could depend on the deceased, higher-earning spouse's benefits. If you earn more money than your spouse, in other words, it could make sense to hold off on filing for your own benefit so that they will get the highest amount possible if you die.

IF YOU ARE MARRIED …

Married couples often ask how the benefit that one spouse receives will affect how much the other gets. Your marital status does not change how much each of you can receive as individuals based on your separate earnings histories. You can collect those retirement benefits at the same time without any reduction.

You might be able to receive more, however, by instead claiming a spousal benefit, which one spouse receives based on the other's earnings record. The maximum spousal benefit is half of what the other would get at full retirement age. To get that full 50 percent payment, the spouse claiming the benefit also must have reached full retirement age. You can't get both your own retirement benefit and a spousal benefit at the same time. Social Security will pay only the greater of the two.

Let's say your earnings record would give you a retirement benefit of $1,200 a month, and your spouse's record would generate a benefit of $2,000. Your spousal benefit would be half that $2,000, or less than the amount your own earnings record produced. You would get the higher amount of $1,200, and a spousal benefit would not apply. Suppose, though, that your spouse's record generated a benefit of $3,000 at full retirement age, even if they opted to collect earlier. You would get a $1,500 spousal payment instead of your own benefit of $1,200 a month.

A spousal benefit, in short, is not the same as a retirement benefit. It could be greater or lesser. You will get whichever is more, but not both. And the spousal benefit applies only when both are alive. A survivor benefit is calculated differently. If the widow or widower has reached full retirement age, they get 100 percent of the deceased's benefit. It will be a lower amount if the deceased claimed benefits early.[32]

32   Social Security Resource Center, "Does My Spouse's Earnings History Affect My Social Security Retirement Benefit?," AARP, updated June 1, 2021, www.aarp.org/retirement/social-security/questions-answers/spouse-income-affect-social-security-retirement.html.

You also should consider factors that could reduce your Social Security payments. For example, if you choose to file early for benefits at age sixty-two, you will be limited in how much you can continue to earn—and that includes not only wages but also vacation pay, bonuses, and commissions (but not investment income and interest). In 2021, the maximum annual earnings allowed was $18,960. For every two dollars that you earn over the threshold, Social Security deducts a dollar from your benefit. Once you reach full retirement age, you are not limited on how much you can earn. Your benefits will not be reduced.

You may have to pay income tax on the benefits you receive, however. The Social Security Administration says about 40 percent of people who get benefits pay income taxes on them. If Social Security is your only retirement income, you probably will not be taxed, but those who have a moderate income or greater likely will be paying tax on much of what they receive in benefits. In addition, thirteen states also tax Social Security benefits.[33]

Some employers do not withhold Social Security taxes. Some government agencies, schools, and companies located outside the United States may instead offer a pension plan. If you receive a pension from a governmental body or other organization that did not withhold FICA, you could see a reduction in your Social Security benefits, and it could lower spousal benefits as well.

Some of the premiums that you pay for Medicare coverage also will be deducted from your Social Security payments. Your Part B premium will be automatically deducted, and you can choose to have Parts C and D deducted as well. Let's look at the details of how the Medicare program works.

---

33 Vanguard, "How Taxes Can Affect Your Social Security Benefits," accessed September 6, 2021, https://investor.vanguard.com/retirement/social-security/taxes-on-benefits.

Medicare Insights

Nancy was distraught when she discovered a lump in her breast. Confronted with the unknown, she couldn't help but to think the worst. After spending an hour surfing medical sites, desperate for reassurance, she was a wreck. All the horror stories flooded her heart, but she didn't let fear paralyze her. Snapping her laptop shut, she called her doctor for an appointment and then she called us.

"This is pretty much a money disaster, isn't it?" she asked us. "I mean, how can I do this to my family?" She was crying. "Maybe it's best if I go fast!"

We knew Nancy to be levelheaded, a good decision maker. She had been a client for years, and we had transitioned her into a promising retirement. Now, though, the unknown was distorting her thinking, making that bright and active future seem bleak and empty.

We assured her that calling us for help right away had been a wise move and that we would get her some clear answers without delay. "But you know, Nancy, there's a cap on how much you have to pay out of pocket every year under Medicare," we said. "Now, that amount changes every year, but we'll get you the exact figure you need."

We put a call through to our Medicare consultant, who got back to us within minutes. "The most that she would have to pay in 2020 for expenses that are covered by Medicare is $8,150," he said. We relayed that to Nancy, who slowly exhaled, and she was further relieved to later learn the results of the biopsy. The lump was benign.

Two big worries had slammed Nancy at the same time, and they were the ones that retirees say trouble them the most: *Will my health fail? Will my finances fail?* Healthcare costs are the top retirement concern for Americans, a Bankrate survey found.[34] It's another example of the fear of the unknown: Fewer than 15 percent of people nearing retirement age have estimated what their costs will be, according to another survey by Merrill Lynch and Age Wave.[35] No wonder they worry. They have questions, but they lack answers. What they need is reliable information that can help to allay those worries—at least the financial ones.

Medicare is the federal government's health insurance plan for people age sixty-five and older, and the program entails a lot of choices—so many that people often feel stymied in their decision-making. Still, those decisions can't wait.

The program includes several parts with different levels of coverage and premiums. To make the best selections, you need to assess your family's specific needs and preferences. Signing up can feel like a giant task: Is Part A sufficient, or should we pay to add Part B, and why? More than once I have heard people snicker and ask: "To B or not to B? That is the question."

It's not as if folks have practice with these Medicare decisions. They might look for guidance online, but the process is so complex that they still find themselves scratching their heads. They must prioritize their needs and then they have to evaluate all the plan options to see which ones cover those priorities. The selection often requires trade-offs, with affordability a major concern. It requires an estimate of healthcare costs in the future and a projection for the level of protection that would be needed in a worst-case scenario. Invariably, you will have many other questions along the way. For example, what

---

34 Amanda Dixon, "This Is the No. 1 Reason Americans Are Losing Sleep," Bankrate, August 16, 2018, https://www.bankrate.com/personal-finance/smart-money/money-worries-survey-august-2018.

35 Bank of America, "What Are Top Retirement Concerns and How to Address Them," accessed September 6, 2021, https://bettermoneyhabits.bankofamerica.com/en/retirement/top-retirement-concerns.

should you do if you are receiving veteran benefits? Or should you do something different if you and your spouse have a serious existing illness?

After figuring out all of that as best you can, you then get to shop for specific policies among various providers.

Medicare doesn't cover everything—notably, long-term care. Retirees must make separate plans to cover that risk, for which 52 percent of them can expect some expenses. Here's how much retirees might expect to pay for long-term care:[36]

- Forty-eight percent of retirees will have no costs.

- Twenty-five percent will pay up to $100,000.

- Eleven percent will pay between $100,000 and $250,000.

- Fifteen percent of retirees will pay more than $250,000.

Other exceptions also can add up to a lot of money, so you want to know your options and select the parts that are appropriate for you and your family. Parts A and B are parts of the original Medicare plan, but you can add Medigap supplements, provided by private companies that are licensed in your state to sell those policies.

Part A, which covers hospital stays, has no premium if you are sixty-five and you or your spouse have paid taxes for ten years. When you enroll in Part A, you automatically get signed up for Part B. Part B is medical insurance and helps pay for doctors and other health-care providers, outpatient care, home healthcare, durable medical equipment, and some preventive services. However, you must pay for Part B, and the premium is deducted from your Social Security payments. If you choose to pay more for even better coverage, you can opt for Part C, which replaces A and B. Most of the Part C plans

---

36   Vanguard, "Retirement Health Care Costs," accessed September 6, 2021, https://investor.vanguard.com/retirement/planning/retirement-health-care-costs.

have an out-of-pocket maximum and may include dental, hearing, and vision coverage. And then there's Part D. That's a prescription plan that you also can add for a price.[37]

There's a nice simple graphic of the parts on Vanguard's website at https://investor.vanguard.com/retirement/planning/understanding-medicare-parts-a-to-d.

PARTS OF MEDICARE

	COVERS	THE BASICS	YOU SHOULD KNOW
PART **A**	Hospital care costs.	Part of Traditional Medicare run by the U.S. government.	It's free at 65 if you or your spouse have worked (and paid taxes) for 10 years.
PART **B**	Outpatient & doctor visits.	Part of Traditional Medicare run by the U.S. government.	It's not free. Monthly premiums are set annually. You also might have a co-pay.
PART **C**	Hospital & physician costs.	Also known as Medicare Advantage offered by private insurance companies.	Most plans have an out-of-pocket max. They also may cover dental, hearing, and vision costs.
PART **D**	Prescription costs.	Can be added to Traditional Medicare (A+B) or Medicare Advantage (C).	Costs will vary depending on the plan you choose and prescriptions you need.
MEDIGAP	Out-of-pocket costs, such as co-pays and deductibles.	Can be added to Traditional Medicare (A+B) but not Medicare Advantage (C).	You can get Medigap later, but you might pay more for services.

SOURCE: *https://investor.vanguard.com/retirement/planning/understandingmedicare-parts-a-to-d.*

---

37 For more on Medicare costs, visit www.medicare.gov/your-medicare-costs/ medicare-costs-at-a-glance.

If your income is low enough, you can qualify for Medicaid. But once you turn sixty-five, you must enroll in Medicare. If you don't do it during your enrollment period, you will be financially penalized. If you are receiving Social Security benefits at age sixty-five, you will automatically be enrolled into Medicare, even if you are working. Some people don't realize that Medicare requires a monthly charge. Most people don't pay for Part A of Medicare because they paid for it with Medicare taxes when they were working. In 2021, the standard Part B plan for most people costs $148.50 per month. That is for individuals earning no more than $88,000 and married couples earning no more than $176,000. The cost goes up at higher income levels, rising to $504.90 for individuals earning half a million or more.

In short, most people who choose to pay for only Part B will face an expense of a couple thousand dollars a year. If you add in typical costs of Parts C and D, the annual expense could be around $5,000. If you have a portfolio of a million dollars, those costs are not much as a percentage. But don't forget those out-of-pocket costs for expenses related to healthcare that are above and beyond what Medicare will cover. Again, the findings of the Fidelity study: A couple retiring in 2021 at age sixty-five typically may need to have saved $300,000, after taxes, to pay for those costs in the years ahead. That is getting close to a third of the value of a portfolio worth a million dollars.

What matters most is awareness. For all of your retirement costs, you should know what is likely to lie ahead. Those calculations should be in place before you finalize a decision to retire.

HEALTH SAVINGS ACCOUNTS

A health savings account (HSA) is unique in the world of tax-preferred investment accounts because it is currently the only type of account that allows you to benefit from both tax-deductible contributions and tax-free distributions. That differs from, for example, traditional IRAs or 401(k)s, which can reduce your taxable income for the year in which you make the contribution but require you to pay the taxes when you make withdrawals.

Unlike IRAs or 401(k)s, which require distributions, you can keep money in an HSA for as long as you want. The money is available for you to spend on qualified medical expenses either now or way into the future. That means the money in these accounts can grow tax-free for a long time. If the HSA has not been used by the time the owner dies, the surviving spouse can gain control of the account and maintain the same benefits. Because of those unique tax advantages, some people pay out of pocket for medical expenses that arise early in retirement so that the money in the HSA will continue to compound and grow.

The qualified expenses for which you can use an HSA include deductibles, copayments, and other medical expenses. (For a full list, see IRS Publication 502.) The tax break on those expenses effectively lowers your overall healthcare costs.

To qualify for an HSA, you must be enrolled in what is considered a high-deductible health plan, which for 2021 means a deductible of $1,400 for self-only coverage and $2,800 for family coverage. (IRS Publication 969 details exceptions.)

The contribution limit for 2021 is $3,600 for individuals or $7,200 for couples. There is a catch-up provision for people who are age fifty-five or over. Those amounts are expected to

increase. An HSA gives you the potential to accumulate significant savings to pay for medical expenses during retirement, free
of income tax. And it's convenient. Most HSAs issue a debit
card to pay for those qualified expenses, or you can pay in cash
and reimburse yourself.

CHAPTER 6

HOW THE RICH AVOID TAXES AND YOU CAN, TOO

<hr>

Anyone may so arrange his affairs that his taxes shall be as low as possible; he is not bound to choose that pattern which will best pay the Treasury; there is not even a patriotic duty to increase one's taxes.
—US JUDGE LEARNED HAND (1872–1961)

IF YOU CAN AVOID INCOME, you can avoid taxes. That's how the wealthiest among us have sidestepped the tax system, perfectly legally, and you can use their strategies to do the same, particularly if you own a business.

As I was writing this book, thousands of confidential tax returns were anonymously handed to the nonprofit news organization Pro-Publica. These tax records show how billionaires such as Jeff Bezos, Carl Icahn, Elon Musk, Michael Bloomberg, and George Soros have bypassed taxation. Bezos even claimed a $4,000 tax credit in 2011 when he claimed zero income.

ProPublica said it was in the public's best interests to report that billionaires were able to pay as little as zero federal income taxes in some years. I say it's in the best interests of America to tell my fellow small business owners how they can, too.

The highest federal income tax rate in 2021 is 37 percent. According to the ProPublica information, the "true tax rate" of the richest twenty-five Americans was 3.4 percent between 2014 and 2018 when you consider not only income but also how much their wealth appreciated in those years.

Though I disagree with ProPublica's math, the information still makes a strong point. The tax maneuvers of the ultrarich are highly effective. They have ways to pay only a fraction of what normal wage earners pay in taxes. You might not be able to use these tax-saving tips today. We have all heard the expression it takes money to make money. It also takes money to not pay money. Nonetheless, these are tactics that ordinary people routinely use.

The lesson for business owners essentially is this: The best path to wealth is to fund your company's growth instead of triggering a taxable event. The easiest way to think about this is that you want to gain access to tax-free money. The tax code favors those who make money from investments that are taxed only when they are sold.

Most Americans predominantly receive income through wages or salaries (known as "labor income"). Business owners, however, receive income through capital gains, rents, or dividends (those payments are known as "capital income"). Typically, the more profitable your company, the greater your opportunity to increase your percentage of capital income. Because labor income is typically taxed at higher rates, that ratio allows business owners to reduce their effective tax rate.

Access to wealth means not having to live off paychecks. Many business owners don't receive regular paychecks. They have the flexibility to take income only when they have losses to offset it. Or they can sell stock or other assets that are taxed at a lower rate. The ultrarich often don't take any income or sell any assets. Instead, they borrow against their assets and use that loan money to pay bills or invest outside of the business, or in it.

Here are the three primary strategies the ultrarich use—and you can, too.

Strategy #1: Offsetting Gains with Losses

Stock investors often declare losses to offset their gains. It's the common practice of tax-loss harvesting: they can sell some securities that have lost value, which reduces the amount of capital gains tax on their winners.

With wealth comes the advantage of determining when to realize gains from a stock sale. The wealthy can use their investment portfolio as a cash source instead of a salary or dividends. With more control over the timing, they can use losses to offset gains to the greatest advantage, thus avoiding as much tax as possible. The money that would have gone to the government instead can stay in the portfolio to be compounded over time.

Even when investors have no losses to claim, they still have the opportunity to pay only the 20 percent long-term capital gains tax rate—well below the 37 percent rate of the highest bracket of ordinary income tax.[38] Growing an investment portfolio provides another source of income. If done right, it makes the higher income tax rate voluntary.

---

38   These are the capital gains and ordinary income tax rates in effect in 2021.

Strategy #2: Borrowing

How can the ordinary person reduce taxes by borrowing money? Here are two common ways: homeowners can borrow against their homes with a mortgage and deduct the interest payments, and investors can buy stocks on margin.

The ultrarich borrow against their wealth. For example, Musk pledged Tesla shares as collateral to borrow billions of dollars. Icahn acknowledged that he is a "big borrower" and that his effective tax rate was low because his "interest was higher than [his] whole adjusted income."

Small business owners can access millions of dollars without producing income or selling stock, thus avoiding paying a tax. They could take out a bank loan at a single-digit interest rate and pay no tax while deducting the interest on the payments. Larry Ellison, the CEO of Oracle and one of the world's richest people, used a technique like that to access a credit line secured by about $10 billion of his shares.

Borrowed money is a way to avoid taxable events such as selling an asset or taking a distribution, or to postpone those events till a better time. The cost of the loan is less than the taxes that otherwise would be paid. And once you pay off that loan, you're probably an even better lending risk.

Business owners also can use those loans to invest in their business. Think about the beauty in this. Say you want to expand your operations and open a satellite office. Instead of selling an appreciated property and paying the taxes, you can use that property to secure a loan to

Don't be afraid of debt. Used properly, it can help to build wealth.

make new investments. So while you pay off tax-deductible interest, your investment continues to appreciate. The deductions bring down your effective tax rate while your wealth grows. Don't be afraid of debt. Used properly, it can help to build wealth.

By using the bank's money to own your property, you also can own more things—cars, buildings, machines. And when you own more things, you can depreciate them on your tax return. You don't spend any money, but you pay less in taxes.

Another strategy involves insurance products: Your business can take out a life insurance policy with a high cash dividend on yourself and your key employees. The premium payments are tax deductible, lowering your effective tax rate. A bank will collateralize that asset and let you borrow against it. In both cases, it is effectively income to you, but it is not considered by the IRS to be income or a capital gain, so it is tax-free money.

If real estate is your pleasure, one way to avoid taxation is a like-kind exchange, by which you could defer taxes for life. The provision allows you to sell an asset and acquire a similar one without generating a capital gains tax liability from the sale.

If you have the money, you can hire a team to create a financial derivative contract called an "equity swap." An equity swap allows you and someone else to agree to an exchange of assets at set dates in the future to avoid transactions costs, including local taxes.

Strategy #3: Charitable Gifting

Every year, millions of Americans donate to charity. It's one of the more common ways of reducing taxes. Donations, however, don't always mean giving away your assets so that you can't make use of them. Here are several examples of how charitable contributions can be used creatively as a means of avoiding or reducing taxes:

- A landowner can receive a tax deduction when the IRS grants a conservation easement in exchange for agreeing to leave portions of the land undeveloped. The land may later be appraised significantly above the acquisition price. Or you could buy a sculpture for $1 million and later have it appraised for ten times that amount. You could then donate the sculpture and deduct that $10 million against your income.

- You can open a charitable remainder trust (CRT) or a donor-advised fund (DAF). You can make a tax-deductible contribution into a CRT or DAF, and it will eventually go to a charity of your choice. Until then, the account provides you an income stream. Before the sale of a business is a good time to consider a CRT or DAF. For many people, the year they sell their business is the most significant tax year of their lives. You could place some of the appreciated company stock in the account to avoid paying taxes on that portion of the sale. You still get the tax deduction and the income.

- With a retained life estate, you can donate your house, or other residences, to a qualified charity, but you can still live there for the rest of your life.

Are Taxes Killing Your Business?

Those are some of the ways the ultrarich reduce their taxes, and those same strategies could be available to all business owners. From time to time, however, politicians move to close what some consider loopholes in tax policy that favor the wealthy. As I write this chapter, for example, one such proposal would double the long-term capital gains tax for investors making over $1 million, to 39.6 percent from 20 percent. Capital gains would be taxed like ordinary income.

Now suppose you are a small business owner preparing to sell your company and retire. You might not ever have made a million dollars even in your best year, but you expect to sell for $10 million. Under that proposal, the additional tax would vaporize nearly $2 million of your after-tax proceeds. You might not be among the mega-wealthy, but you still could stand to lose mega-dollars to taxes.

Under any circumstances, smart business owners see it as an imperative to reduce their tax burden. Remember: *You only pay taxes on profit*, so you should be claiming every expense. IRS Form 8829 allows you to deduct home office expenses such as mortgage interest, real estate taxes, utilities, and depreciation. Be sure to claim technology, supplies, cell phone, and business travel. Your expenses, however, shouldn't consistently exceed your revenues. Some owners have told me that they take any "profit" and invest it back into the company. However, all that means is that their company doesn't make any money, and it is essentially worthless.

You can help yourself and your employees by finding a noncash means to compensate them. If you pay your employee with wages, then they must pay income tax. Both the owner and the employee must pay FICA (Federal Insurance Contributions Act) and Medicare tax, a total of 7.65 percent each. Add employee benefits instead of raises. For example, add an equivalent amount of additional medical insurance or college reimbursement.

You can take your pretax money and sock it away into tax-deferred investment accounts. You reduce your taxes while building your retirement portfolio.

Contributing to a qualified plan reduces taxable self-employment income. Assume your taxable self-employment income without a qualifying plan contribution is $300,000. If you contribute $50,000 into a qualified plan, your taxable income reduces to $250,000. That lower income triggers fewer tax payments elsewhere. It won't affect your Social Security taxes because you have to pay up to the first $142,800 of income in 2021. But you'll pay $1,450 less on Medicare taxes (2.9 percent), and your additional Medicare tax on self-employment income would drop to zero because it is assessed only on income of more than $250,000. Your federal income tax amount would be reduced by nearly $20,000, making it roughly a 16 percent drop of your tax cost.

A SEP-IRA allows business owners to shield up to $58,000 per year (2021 limits). SEP stands for Simplified Employee Pension. It provides the benefits of a traditional IRA in terms of ownership and taxation. The downside is that you must make a prorate contribution for employees, and that can be expensive.

A SIMPLE IRA may be a more cost-effective option than a SEP-IRA. SIMPLE stands for Savings Incentive Match Plan for Employees. Like the SEP, the SIMPLE IRA avoids complex federal reporting requirements that are typical for a 401(k). The SIMPLE decrees that employers offer a match (for example, on the employee's contributions up to 3 percent of wages). Contributions are limited to $13,500 (2021 limit), and the employees are responsible for their contributions, other than the match.

A health savings account (HSA), as explained in chapter 5, enables you to deflect up to $7,200 of income per year (2021 limit) from taxes. An HSA is unique because you benefit from both the tax-deductible contributions and the federally tax-free distributions. The

HSA allows you to use untaxed money for costs such as deductibles, copayments, and other medical expenses.

A defined benefit plan can be either a cash balance plan or a pension plan. Participants in a defined benefit plan can contribute up to $230,000 per year in 2021. Instead of paying taxes on $2.3 million over the next decade ($230,000 × ten years, assuming no increases), you put that money into a retirement account. A business owner and a spousal employee can "front load" a contribution and protect nearly $900,000 of income. Defined benefit plans, like 401(k)s, also can permit loans.

The pension version of defined benefit plans has become less popular as large corporations have reduced their legacy costs. The cash balance version is similar, but instead of providing an annuity payment, employees get a lump sum.

IRS Publication 3998 (Rev. 11-2020) offers additional retirement solutions and more details so that you can shield your company from taxes.[39]

It's your responsibility to maximize your success by minimizing your taxes. Higher taxes will make your company less valuable, but these strategies can help you get ahead in retirement.

Consider this basic calculation: A $100,000 portfolio will grow to $672,750 in twenty years if compounded annually at 10 percent. However, if that portfolio is subjected to a 40 percent tax rate during those years, the result will be a portfolio of roughly half that

> Strategies to reduce tax liability can go a long way toward protecting your money.

---

39 Employee Benefits Security Administration, "Choosing a Retirement Solution for Your Small Business," November 2020, www.irs.gov/pub/irs-pdf/p3998.pdf.

value. It's as if you suffered a major market crash, except markets typically come roaring back. When taxes are doing the damage, your portfolio just keeps sucking wind.

Strategies to reduce tax liability can go a long way toward protecting your money. In this book, we have been looking at taxation from the perspective of estate planning, income planning, and virtually every aspect of financial management. Much of the strategy involves investing with tax efficiency. As just one example, when a bond fund is part of an IRA account, you don't have to pay ordinary income tax on dividends and interest. Putting the right securities in the right accounts, and withdrawing money from the appropriate accounts, not only can help to build wealth significantly but also can keep taxation to a minimum.

This book couldn't hope to cover all the elements of tax management. The IRS code is thousands of pages long, and it's less than exciting reading material. And because tax laws often change, tax advice ages poorly. That uncertainty can be frustrating and prevents many families from taking a proactive approach to tax planning, and therein lies the biggest risk of all. If you don't plan, you lose.

CHAPTER 7

THE RETIREMENT YOU ENVISION

——————————o-0-=-0——————————

MY MOTHER ISN'T ONE to spend time in a rocking chair. She would rather recondition a rocking chair. By the time she was sixty-three, she was aching to retire, as my dad had done several years earlier. Though she was eager to close the curtains on her career, her show was far from over. Mom was ready for her second act.

First, we had to solve a problem that stops many people from retiring when they wish. Medicare doesn't kick in until age sixty-five, so they keep plugging away just to keep their employer's health insurance. It wasn't easy, but we found a way to close that gap so Mom could retire early.

The next question was how she would fill all those newfound hours. She was adamant about how she would *not* fill them—namely, at the office—but what would she do with all that time on her hands? Having worked with so many retirees who struggle with that question, I think I was more concerned about the matter than she was.

I figured she could use some help finding things to do. Mom and Dad joined us on a couple Harris family vacations to Hilton

Head and Disney. That took care of twenty days. And I knew she liked to garden, so maybe that would keep her busy—for a few hours a week and part of the year.

Mom rose to the challenge. She began going to tag sales and antique shops where she would buy old pieces of furniture and then she would buy the materials to refurbish them. She set up a workbench in the garage and fitted it out with everything she needed. At first, she and Dad placed her creations around the house. Some of them found their way to my sister's house. One day when I stopped to visit, Mom was at her workbench surrounded by her handiwork. In fact, so many of her finished projects were packed and stacked in the garage that I felt like an acrobat as I tried to get through to see her.

We decided to sell some of it and found that there was a demand for her work. She was producing attractive furniture that people wanted. After years in a career working with cash and inventory, she now had a creative outlet. She went into business as Garage Gal Vintage, and though her overhead was expensive, it all worked out to her advantage.

Mom wasn't looking for a job. She found a hobby and then realized she could make some money doing it. She not only was filling her hours with something that she enjoyed but also found a way to help preserve all those years of retirement savings that she would need to maintain her lifestyle.

The Second Act

Though many people anticipate retirement as a time when they will not be working anymore, they soon discover that all that leisure time isn't as joyful as they imagined. They get tired of puttering around the house and run out of projects to keep them occupied. They enjoy watching the grandkids now and then, but that still leaves ample time to feel bored.

A lot of bored people resort to staring at the television, an average of about four and a half hours a day for people aged sixty-five to seventy-four, according to 2019 statistics from the American Time Use Survey by the Bureau of Labor Statistics.[40] That's about twice the average for folks of working age. Meanwhile, the retirees averaged only about fifteen minutes of exercise a day, the survey found. The only positive thing I could say about those findings is that at least watching more TV doesn't cost them much—unless they start subscribing to dozens of pay channels and streaming services.

The good news is that legions of retiring baby boomers have no intention of becoming couch potatoes. They continue to approach life with plenty of energy. Where they need to be careful, however, is how much those activities will cost. Looking for something to do, they often begin spending more money than they had anticipated. They play golf, and not just on weekends anymore. They enroll in classes. They do a lot more traveling. They develop an expanded list of wants and wishes that weren't part of their financial plan.

The additional spending can increase the risk of running out of money during retirement. It's not necessarily the $30,000 once-in-a-lifetime vacation that causes the problem. It's the little things, day after day, that add up. To offset the additional drain on their finances, they may take on another paying job—sometimes out of necessity but often just out of the desire to expand their horizons and to be social. It's only human.

When retirees launch a new working phase of life, we call it their "second act." Generally, it is part-time, and usually they want control

---

40   US Bureau of Labor Statistics, "American Time Use Survey News Release," June 25, 2020, www.bls.gov/news.release/archives/atus_06252020.htm.

over how much effort they put into the endeavor. Many retirees find a way to make money that doesn't involve a boss looking over their shoulder—or, if they do have a boss, they choose work that is less stressful, more social, and more rewarding and fun.

If your intent is to turn a hobby into a money-making venture, plan carefully so that you don't generate debt instead. Treat what you do as a business. Think about the funding, expenses, revenue, and tax considerations so that your endeavors don't end up leaking money. Your goal is to make a profit. Success is a lot more fun.

In other words, count the costs of whatever you pursue in retirement. Your golden years should be satisfying and enjoyable, so congratulations every time you switch off the TV. Nonetheless, always compare and contrast your retirement dreams with your ability to financially sustain them. You want your second act to get rave reviews.

Up from the Rocking Chair

Dreams don't come true spontaneously. They require planning. Whether your idea of retirement is to travel, volunteer for a charity, start a small business, write a book, or spend more time with your kids and grandkids, you will need to schedule the time and use it well. Most people entering retirement have decades of good living ahead of them and exciting opportunities to pursue, but goals that go unplanned, whether big or small, tend to be goals that don't happen.

Unfortunately, many people don't prepare, and it's the emotional adjustment more than the financial considerations that can be most troubling. Some envision retirement as a time to relax, others as a time to explore. Neither endless leisure nor endless adventure is realistic, of course. Too much idle time, like too many mint juleps on the porch, will make anyone feel unbalanced. When reality fails to meet expectations, disillusionment sets in.

What retirees do get is more control over their time, which they can use wisely or wastefully. They have much more discretion over when to get up, when to eat, when to work, when to play, and when to sleep. That might sound like a delightful change of pace, an ascent to freedom, but a lot of people find it unnerving. They functioned better with structure.

Couples who enter retirement without preparing themselves emotionally often find the stress takes a toll on their relationship. Togetherness isn't necessarily bliss—do they really want to spend all day in constant companionship? Instead, each should maintain a level of independence, pursuing their own interests. Most couples manage to adjust, as many did during the coronavirus pandemic. They have gone through other major changes in life that can be both exciting and unsettling—getting married, having children, buying a house, switching careers. They can navigate the emotional challenges of retirement, too. It calls for an extra measure of understanding.

Don't be surprised if you find yourself wishing you could go back to work. It's a common feeling. As much as people may complain about the workday routine, they find it gives them a sense of stability. In retirement, they may feel isolated. Those who return to work often do so not out of necessity, nor out of boredom. They do so to get back a feeling of connection. The workplace gives many people their sense of identity. Once they leave it, and no longer regularly see their friends and associates, they may feel empty inside.

That's why retirees commonly stay on the job part-time. Others serve as consultants or as mentors to younger people, sharing their life and career experience. They also can find gratification in volunteering their time in service to causes or institutions. They accept positions on charitable and community boards or run for political office. Those who reach out in such ways don't often complain that they are bored. They may even wonder how they ever had time to hold down a full-time job. Sure, they enjoy relaxing, but they have no intention of just watching the world go by.

A Purposeful Portfolio

Retirees see life far differently than younger people, who typically focus on developing a career, starting a family, buying a house, and building a future. And then comes a day when that future is now. The focus must shift from building to preserving, and those who fail to make that adjustment are putting their retirement in peril.

For young people, the years stretch ahead, seemingly without end. If they are wise, they begin to save and invest so that money can compound through the decades. If they suffer a setback, they figure they can weather it. Time is on their side. As retirement nears, however, the concerns of life change, and they become more protective of the savings that must sustain them.

> Protecting money requires an entirely different discipline than saving money.

They feel more vulnerable to the toll of inflation, taxes, health issues, and anything else that could threaten their nest egg.

Protecting money requires an entirely different discipline than saving money. As they get older, people tend to invest increasingly more conservatively. No longer do they figure they can risk a loss and still be all right for the long haul. They become more focused on damage prevention and control.

It's not just about money, though. Older people also increasingly focus on their legacy. This is a stage of life when they catch their breath and ponder the why of their endeavors. *What is life all about? How will we be remembered?* They want to pass on not just money but values, too. They reflect on where they have been, where they expect to go, and why. What was the point of setting those savings aside? Was it just to spend, or could they use it to do something meaningful in the world?

A portfolio should have a purpose. Life is far from over, so it is time to take stock of what matters most. It's time to get a clear picture of your values, goals, and relationships. Are you living the life that you want to live? Who and what are most important to you? What would your best life look like? Those are questions that can determine the difference between aging aimlessly and aging gracefully.

As the hair grows grayer, those considerations feel more urgent. In a survey of what matters most to retirees, those who identified themselves as happiest also emphasized the importance of giving back, according to research reported by the Wharton School of the University of Pennsylvania. Desiring to leave a meaningful legacy, they proceed with a sense of purpose. Money matters, but the happiest retirees have more than an investment plan. They have a plan to stay engaged and productive, using their talents and passions in service to others. They want to keep contributing.[41]

For many people, what gets in the way is a lack of confidence. In an early 2020 survey by the Employee Benefit Research Institute, about a quarter of retirees and nearly a third of the workforce lacked confidence that they would have enough money to live comfortably. In a March follow-up during the pandemic, retirees felt slightly less

---

41   The Wharton School, "The Retirement Problem: What Will You Do with All That Time?," January 14, 2016, https://knowledge.wharton.upenn.edu/article/the-retirement-problem-what-will-you-do-with-all-that-time.

confident, but more than half of workers who had experienced job cutbacks doubted they would have enough for their retirement.[42]

The same survey, however, also found that only four of every ten workers and six in ten retirees had ever tried to calculate their retirement income needs. Much of the worry, in other words, stems from the unknown. Without a clear picture of what you will need, how can you gauge whether you will have enough to retire? How can you tell whether you are being too extravagant or too frugal?

> Without a clear picture of what you will need, how can you gauge whether you will have enough to retire?

One should never rule out a dream before knowing what is possible. Don't decide that you can't help others because you aren't sure whether you can help yourself. Yes, we each must live within our means. You stay out of trouble by never spending more than you can afford. The key is knowing how much you can afford. With financial planning, you gain clarity and confidence that you won't run out of money—and you might well discover that you have more means than you imagined.

A Word for the Women

In America it is common for the husband to be solely in charge of handling the household finances, including preparing for retirement. That's unfortunate because both spouses should be involved. After all, they will be going through retirement as a team. We're creating a

---

42 Employee Benefit Research Institute, "2020 Retirement Confidence Survey Summary Report," April 23, 2020, www.ebri.org/docs/default-source/rcs/2020-rcs/2020-rcs-summary-report.pdf?sfvrsn=84bc3d2f_7.

plan for both spouses, not just one, and so we develop a rapport with the families we serve. They sometimes invite us to weddings. We have been pallbearers at funerals. And we participate in family meetings where we talk about goals and the financial arrangements that would be required to meet them.

What we find when we speak to both spouses is that they often differ on how their retirement world should look. Seldom have they had meaningful conversations to make sure that they are on the same page with their expectations. Their perspectives may be quite different—and they don't necessarily know it. One spouse may be keen on traveling. The other may want to devote much of the couple's savings to launching a business. One may want to leave money to the children. The other may think the kids have enough money or that they can't be trusted with it. To forestall friction, couples need to talk about it.

It's not unusual that the wife doesn't have the information to know whether she will be all right financially if her husband dies. He hasn't filled her in on very much. If he dies before her, which is the more likely scenario, one of the children often takes control of things for Mom. She switches to the son's or daughter's advisor, and a new professional relationship has to start from scratch.

Although everyone should take an active lifelong interest in their financial affairs, women have a particularly acute need to do so. They trail behind men in their retirement resources, according to a report from the National Institute on Retirement Security. Contributing to that difference, the study found, were such factors as the wage gap throughout a woman's career, the time that she spent in caregiving, and the financial drain of divorce.[43]

---

43   Christian E. Weller, Joelle Saad-Lessler, and Tyler Bond, "Still Shortchanged: An Update on Women's Retirement Preparedness," National Institute on Retirement Security, May 2020, www.nirsonline.org/reports/stillshortchanged.

Specifically, the study reported that women, having earned less in their careers, were able to save less. They live longer, so their savings must last longer, and they face higher healthcare costs as they age. They also are more likely to be widowed, and the household savings may have been depleted by the husband's healthcare costs before he died. Also, women's Social Security benefits tend to be less because of years when they left the workforce to care for their children or aging parents. Many women also find it harder to recover financially from a divorce.

The facts speak loudly of the need for women to take early measures to protect their future livelihood and enhance their savings for retirement. They need to be smart about the family finances and involved at every step. Couples tend to divide household responsibilities in traditional ways—one of which is leaving the financial oversight to the man. He may feel he is protecting his wife from a ton of worries by handling it all himself. It doesn't work that way. Couples must talk about how money works in their relationship and how they envision their spending and income in retirement.

If You Own a Business

In my book *Build It, Sell It, Profit,* I specifically address the retirement concerns of business owners. When it comes time to sell, or to transfer the operations to the kids, what should they do? What should they be doing now?

Unsure of how to prepare for retirement, many business owners just keep on keeping on. They focus their attention on what they know how to do well. They are sophisticated and knowledgeable about their industry, but often they need to fill a gap in their understanding when it comes to making the most of everything that they have worked so hard to build.

As a Certified Exit Planning Advisor, I can help those business owners prepare for the next steps in life, including helping to sell the company for the highest possible price. I have attained the specialized training and credentials to assist with the details of the exit, although what I do involves much more than that. I also help business owners attend to the building stages of their business, which must start sooner rather than later. Getting started now on the process of planning for an eventual sale or transfer will help business owners to clarify just where they stand and what they need to do today.

Business owners have the same big question as anyone anticipating retirement: *Will I have enough money?* The big answer: *That depends on what you want to do next.* Without knowing the next step in life, you cannot know whether your resources will be sufficient to generate the necessary income to support your lifestyle. And unless you can project those requirements, you cannot know the best way to invest your money to meet them.

While maximizing the growth of the business, the owner must prepare for the life that they envision. Both are important objectives. Solid financial and exit planning provides the sense of direction needed to make progress. It starts with numbers and it ends with numbers, and along the way it takes a hard look at life. To what will those numbers be assigned? I ask about dreams and goals so that together we can run the math and see whether we can design a plan to support those objectives.

It can be hard to say goodbye. Business owners may feel as if they are giving up part of their identity when they finally sell. For years, perhaps decades, the identity of the owner and the business have been inseparable. It's a bittersweet parting. The owner feels ties to the community and wants the business to continue taking good care of their employees and friends who have been loyal for so long.

In return for reassurance that the business will be in good hands, the owner may be willing to settle for fewer dollars from the deal. The owner, for example, may want to hand over the business to their children or even to trusted senior managers for a value that is far less than what the market would provide. It's not just about the money.

Often, the sale is structured so that the seller will stick around and continue working in the business for a while with some sort of continuing compensation agreement. For the seller, the ostensible reason generally is to help the new management adjust to the transition. The buyer may demand that arrangement to reduce risk. But often it is just as much a case of helping the seller adjust to the transition. They sign the papers but still come to work every day, perhaps as a consultant. The goodbye is gradual.

All too often, though, the parting is poorly planned. Business owners often fall short when it comes to developing a retirement portfolio. They could do a good job, but they don't. According to the Exit Planning Institute, often 80 to 90 percent of a business owner's net worth is tied up in the company.[44] What they sacrifice is the lifestyle that they might have had in the years to come. It's good to grow the business, but that isn't enough because the business isn't a liquid resource.

As they get older, many business owners increasingly feel that they would like to sell and move on to something else in life, but they are not sure what, and they don't know how to proceed. Surveys have shown that most business owners do not know their exit options—they don't know how to get the documentation together and present

---

44 Exit Planning Institute, "The State of Owner Readiness Research," accessed September 6, 2021, https://exit-planning-institute.org/state-of-owner-readiness.

the sale, and they don't know who might help them. They want out, but they don't know how to get out.

The concept of retirement seems comforting from a thirty-thousand-foot view, but many people feel intimidated once they are coming in for the landing and see the details of the landscape. This is new territory. It is the unknown. Many people find it easier to just keep on working rather than try to figure it all out on their own. If they did cash in on the business, they wonder, would it be enough to retire on? After all, they have little in the way of other savings and investments. At least the business is providing an income for now, they figure. And so they keep on working—and worrying.

It is what you do not know that can be most troubling. Business owners need to consult with someone who understands them and who has experience in money management and exit planning. Knowledge builds confidence. And confidence leads to action.

CHAPTER 8

MANAGING YOUR ESTATE

SAM AND SARAH had been convinced that their two little girls, both on the autism spectrum, would need a lifetime of care, so the couple set up an irrevocable special needs trust to provide for them. As the years passed, the girls began exhibiting a remarkable ability to adapt and cope. They showed the promise of becoming independent young women.

"We're delighted they're doing so well," Sam told us when the couple came in to talk about the matter, "but this raises the question of those provisions in the trust directing money to be used only for their caretaking. I mean, isn't irrevocable, like, *irrevocable?*"

We assured him that there were ways to dissolve the old trust and replace it with a new one spelling out their wishes.

"But even if we do that," Sarah asked, "what if one decides to go to college and the other just isn't able to get that far? We want to make it fair for both." We referred them to a legal specialist who helped them redirect the assets of the trust and fulfill their vision, including an education equalizer clause to ensure that each daughter would receive fair and equal financial support.

Another couple came to us concerned about leaving money to their children who were spendthrifts. "The dollars just slip through their fingers, and they won't be able to handle an inheritance," the husband told us.

"That's right," his wife added, "and we're worried that nothing will be left to take care of our grandkids."

We explained that many people have such anxieties. The solution for their situation was a trust that, upon their passing, would regulate their children's spending of their inheritance while also providing generously for the grandchildren.

Those are examples of estate planning, which is crucial at every stage in life for all families, whether wealthy or not. At Berkshire Money Management, our first step is to identify the client's need and, usually, a solution. Then we set up meetings with estate planning counsel with whom we partner to produce the necessary documents. We attend those meetings, and we follow up to see that the course of action that we worked out with the client is effectively implemented.

What It Is, What It Isn't

If you ask most folks what estate planning is, they might say it's a way to save a lot of money on taxes and expenses when someone dies. And that's true. They might add that estate planning makes it quicker and easier to settle the matter of who gets what. Sure, it can do all that and more, but those answers don't get to the essence of what estate planning is all about.

To contemplate one's own death, or the death of loved ones, isn't easy but it's essential, and we make sure our clients have given due consideration to what will become of their estate. Who will take the reins? At some point in that conversation, clients begin telling us about their children and grandchildren and what they are pursuing in life, for better or for worse. They are so proud of them, or so worried, or so disappointed. "It looks like our Sally is going places!" one couple might say. Another might lament that their Tommy seems lost in a fog of addictions.

And that's when they begin to tap into the true purpose of estate planning. It's about passing on not only possessions and valuables but also one's values. It's natural to want your children and grandchildren to use an inheritance in a way that will uphold the principles that you tried to instill in them.

Your legacy is not as simple as a plaque on a wall or your name on a wing of the museum. Your legacy will be measured instead by how well you protected the members of your family so they can continue to do meaningful things in the world. To do that right, you must prepare. You must get the pieces in place. That's what estate planning does. It protects your family both financially and emotionally. It can forestall the lengthy, grueling, expensive, and public process that otherwise could ensue. It brings clarity to your heirs about your final wishes.

Nobody wants to think it will happen in their family, but ugly legal fights are not uncommon after a family member passes. The clarity of a well-designed estate plan helps to dispel any hard feelings that might not split a family apart but could lead to years of lingering tensions. That strife may be rooted in money, in principle, or in sentiment.

For all the good it can do, money can be divisive. Some relatives may feel they deserve more of an inheritance than they are getting. What feels fair to one person is a farce to another. Celebrity estate battles are a staple in the news, as people crawl out of the woodwork to claim a share. Often, though, the disputes are less about money and more about principle. For example, why was the family business left to all the siblings when only one of them had anything to do with it? Or why did one sibling get money while another inherited a house, along with the maintenance costs and the hassle of selling it?

And very often, the hard feelings arise from sentimental jealousies. *Who Gets Grandma's Yellow Pie Plate?* by Marlene S. Stum is a workbook and program that is well known in the world of estate planning.[45] In her family, she wrote, the pie plate holds a lot of special memories: "It belonged to my great-grandmother, who spent a lot of time in the kitchen with her daughters." The plate might not bring a dollar at a yard sale, yet it came to represent priceless years of love and laughter. So which sister gets the honor of baking up more memories? Decisions like that are tough, and most families can empathize. Maybe it's a baseball glove, or a stamp collection, or Grandpa's fishing pole. Anything dear to the heart can become a source of hurt, and such matters must be handled with delicacy.

As you can see, estate planning doesn't just save on taxes. It can save families.

Dealing with Your Stuff

Your estate is your "stuff," the big and the small. It's your house, savings, car, furniture, and jewelry as well as items whose value is mostly of a sentimental nature. You might say that estate planning is just instructions stating who will get what, but an essential part of the equation also is how they get it. Estate planning helps to transfer

---

45   Marlene S. Stum, *Who Gets Grandma's Yellow Pie Plate? Workbook: A Guide to Passing on Personal Possessions* (St. Paul, MN: University Extension Services, 2011).

those assets as efficiently as possible. If you make the wrong moves, you could bequeath far more than necessary to the IRS.

Through estate planning, you can keep your assets out of probate court. That is the public process for distributing property when no other provisions have been made. It can be expensive and prolonged. But estate planning isn't just about saving money for your family. It's about helping your family in general.

Estate planning instructs how you should be cared for if you become disabled or incapacitated. It arranges for the care and guardianship of your minor children if they have no other parent. If you have a family member with special needs, estate planning can provide for them after you are gone. It includes insurance planning to pay for lost income or to cover taxes. If you own a business, estate planning arranges for the transfer of ownership and roles. And it can protect you from creditors.

Estate planning, in short, protects your wealth, your family, and your legacy. You are deciding how you will pass your estate to loved ones when you want and the way you want.

Before immersing yourself in the details, however, ask yourself questions such as these: What is your vision for your family? How do you want to be remembered? If you have a business, what do you see happening with it? Will it stay in the family, and if so, who will operate it? How will your money serve the generations to come? Do you want to leave money to your children and grandchildren? Do you expect that it will help them, or do you fear that it could hurt them? Will they use it wisely or wantonly?

How you answer such questions will have much to do with the decisions that you make to implement your plans. Your first questions shouldn't be: *Should I have a will or a trust?* or *Should I have this trust or that trust?* Instead, open up to your advisor and let loose that stream of consciousness about your family, your concerns about them, what you want to do for them, and what you want your legacy to look like. Just talk and hold nothing back. Then let your advisor determine the best tools to use to accomplish what you want.

ESTATE PLANNING TOOLS

The following is a brief summary of the common estate planning documents:

- A **will** is the primary way that assets pass to heirs. Upon your death, your executor files the document in probate court, which verifies it as valid. The court ensures that all taxes, debts, and other obligations are satisfied and then distributes your assets as you have directed. The will also can arrange for guardianship of minor children.

- A **revocable living trust** can manage your assets when you're alive, even if you're incapacitated. When you die, the assets in the trust are distributed according to the document's terms. Those assets no longer are considered part of your taxable estate and do not go through probate court. You can add detailed provisions to maintain an influence over your heirs, potentially for generations.

- A **durable power of attorney for finances** is granted to a trusted person to act on your behalf on financial matters if you become incapacitated, to the extent that you have allowed in the document.

- A **healthcare power of attorney** is granted to a trusted person to make medical decisions for you if you can't make them yourself. By giving one person the final say, it can prevent family conflicts.

> - An **advance medical directive, or living will**, sets forth your end-of-life wishes, such as whether you would want doctors to keep you on life support if there was little hope that you could recover and resume a normal life.

The Estate Planning Toolbox

Estate planning depends on the power of several key documents, including wills, trusts, powers of attorney, and advance medical directives. It is not unusual to find that those documents are lacking—inadequate, out of date, or nonexistent. We have come across clients, for example, whose wills provided for the guardianship of children who had long since reached adulthood. We have discovered deceased people named as healthcare proxies. We have seen financial powers of attorney still in place for individuals who were estranged from the family. Not good. I wish I could say that lapses like those are rare. They're not. It's not uncommon for trained professionals to catch such problems.

Let's take a look now into the toolbox of estate planning to see what those key documents can accomplish for you. A qualified attorney needs to draft them to reflect your wishes precisely, but you are the one doing the wishing. By working with a financial advisor who knows you well and acts in your best interests, you can make strides toward developing a solid estate plan to serve your family well.

POWERS OF ATTORNEY

If the time comes when you cannot make decisions for yourself, who will make them for you? You can choose that person by drafting a durable power of attorney for finances. The individual to whom you grant the DPOA will be empowered to handle your affairs if you become incapacitated, whether physically or mentally. They will be able to pay your bills, sign checks, make investment decisions—in short, continue to meet your financial obligations to the extent that you have decided would be appropriate.

Separately, a DPOA for healthcare specifically assigns the authority to make medical decisions for you if you cannot speak for yourself. By legally designating a healthcare proxy who will have the final say on healthcare matters, you can forestall the divisive feelings that often arise when loved ones disagree on the best course of action. Healthcare proxies are legally bound to make those decisions. When it's time to act, they can't just back out and decide they don't want the responsibility.

You may be reluctant to hand over such power over your finances and medical care, fearing it could be abused, but don't worry—these type of DPOAs transfer authorization only under specified conditions. They are known as "springing powers of attorney" in that they spring into effect only during clearly defined situations. Otherwise, the power cannot be exercised.

The alternative to a DPOA is lost time and a lot of aggravation. If you were to become incapacitated, your family would have to go to court and have a form of incompetence declared. The court eventually would assign someone who would be deemed your guardian, and that might not be the person you would have preferred. In the best-case scenario, it can happen fairly quickly with limited costs, but the lack of DPOAs opens the door to family conflict. Someone might try to maneuver to gain control.

Once you have set up the DPOAs, be sure you communicate the breadth of responsibility to the people you have assigned those potential powers. As the agents who might make decisions on your behalf, they need to know their roles, their duties, and the extent of what they would be allowed to do. Then consider consolidating your accounts so that your financial agent can more efficiently contend with those responsibilities.

When you are feeling fit of mind and body, it's tempting to postpone taking care of this responsibility. Here's what often happens: As the years go by, people experience a gradual decline in their acuity. They begin to neglect their financial responsibilities, damaging the estate irreparably before anyone notices or intervenes, to the point where it becomes too late to execute a power of attorney. Or a health crisis comes on suddenly. One day, all seems well. The next, a stroke or an accident leaves them unable to make any such decisions. The bottom line: procrastination can cost a fortune.

ADVANCE MEDICAL DIRECTIVE

Most people are horrified at the prospect of lingering for months or years in a hospital bed, fed through tubes and breathing piped-in oxygen with little hope of recovery. Many would rather die, though some would want to hold out for any chance whatsoever. In an advance medical directive, or living will, you can make your end-of-life wishes known to the doctors and hospital who would be providing your care. You can communicate your desires on pain management and whether you wish to donate organs. Your physicians and hospitals should get copies of the directive. Also give a copy to whoever has the DPOA for healthcare because that is the person who can speak on your behalf on medical issues. The living will does not give anyone the power to speak on your behalf.

WILL

A fundamental of estate planning, your last will and testament is the document in which you declare whom you want to receive your assets and valuables, thereby helping to avoid misunderstandings among heirs. You can leave assets to charity, if you wish, and if you have minor children, you can designate who will take care of them and function as their guardian. The will is essential to every estate plan, and it can be a relatively simple document (particularly if you also have established a living trust, as I will explain in the next section). If you lack a will, you will die intestate, and the court will call the shots. Generally, only your spouse or your closest blood relatives will get anything.

A will does not avoid probate court. In fact, standing alone, a will requires it. That is where the document must land (unless you have minimal assets, as determined by the state). Probate is simply the legal process of administering an estate after death. After the will is confirmed to be legally valid, the court arranges to carry out its instructions and to ensure that all obligations are paid.

An executor whom you have named in the document is responsible for filing it in the probate court upon your death. Working with the court, the executor arranges for the distribution of your assets and belongings in the way you have asked. The executor and court also ensure that all debts, expenses, and taxes have been satisfied before distributing the remainder.

The process can take a few years, or much longer if anyone contests the provisions of the will or files a lawsuit. Someone might claim, for example, that you didn't know what you were doing when you signed your will, or that someone was pressuring you, or that you didn't get enough witnesses or qualified ones. If you own assets in two or more states, you may need to go through multiple probate processes.

Probate also can be expensive, which is a major reason that the process gets a bad reputation. The administrative and professional costs for lawyers, accountants, and others are commonly calculated as a percentage of the total estate value and can add up to several percent of that value.

A client recently came to us with $15 million of taxable money in her own name, which we recommended that she put into a trust to effectively carry out her legacy. That way she also was able to avoid the expenses of probate. To give her an idea of what she was saving, we talked to a lawyer who has often helped people navigate the difficulties of probate court. He estimated that without a trust, her probate costs would have been about $300,000.

Because probate is a court function, the proceedings and filings are open to inspection by the public, including people who believe they should have been included in the will. If your neighbors or a news reporter, for example, might have any interest in pouring over your family affairs, you could find yourself in the spotlight. That may be unlikely—you may be more concerned about keeping your privacy than others are interested in learning about it—but it is a real concern. Probate is public.

If privacy is an issue for you, there are a variety of ways to arrange your estate to keep it out of probate as much as possible, as we will see. Putting assets into a trust is just one way. A will cannot override the beneficiary designation on an insurance policy, retirement account, or annuity. It cannot supersede the deed to a house or take the place of contractual agreements providing for transfer of assets when you die. Those types of transfers do not go to probate court.

TRUSTS

Estate planning might seem to be all about what will happen when you are dead, but you may need strong provisions in place while you are very much alive. Many families have seen a loved one overcome by physical or mental challenges and no longer able to make rational decisions. What happens if you cannot speak for yourself or cope with your financial affairs?

A revocable trust can set in place the particulars of how you want your estate and financial obligations to be managed. It often is called a "living trust" because its provisions include the here and now, not just the hereafter. Your last will and testament can do nothing until you die. A trust, however, takes effect while you are very much alive, even if you are incapacitated. Depending on how you set it up, it can protect against creditors, lawsuits, and divorce claims.

The trust "owns" your assets, but if you function as your own trustee, you can retain the control and management of them while you are alive, and you can change your mind about who should inherit how much, if anything, and under what conditions. You can name a successor trustee to step in and manage all the trust assets after you die or if you become incapacitated. The successor must abide by your instructions as set forth in the trust.

When you die, your heirs generally will get their inheritance much sooner, and since the trust does not go to probate court, the public doesn't get a chance to sort through your laundry.

A trust lets you customize your bequests. When you leave money in a will, or through a beneficiary designation, you are leaving a lump sum. The recipient chooses what to do with the inheritance. Being dead, you can't weigh in on that. However, if you leave money under the terms of a trust, you still can have a say, even from the grave. Some might consider that strategy to be controlling the behavior of the beneficiaries, but think of it as more about protecting and helping them.

Those provisions indeed can regulate how your heirs can spend the money. The trust can parcel it out to them gradually, for example, over the course of their lifetimes. It can provide more to your heirs whom you deem will require more, such as a child with special needs. If you fear an inheritance would render your children lazy, you can stipulate that they get nothing unless they demonstrate that they are gainfully employed. You could even require drug testing or completion of financial education classes. You could arrange to keep money away from someone you think is a gold digger. Or you could set up incentives and pay out generously for specific occasions or accomplishments, such as the purchase of a house, or the launch of a business, or a graduation, or marriage.

For wealthy families, a trust also can help reduce their estate tax. That was a particularly important function when estates were taxed heavily for any value exceeding a federal exemption of a few million dollars. To limit their exposure to the tax, families transferred their assets into a trust. It's less of a concern for most wealthy families today; in 2021, the federal exemption was $11.7 million for an individual and $23.4 million for a married couple. From state to state, however, the estate tax exemption varies. For example, in Massachusetts the threshold is $1 million. And that $1 million exemption does not allow for what's called "portability" between two spouses, so to get the most benefit out of the exemption, the assets should be split between them.

A trust does nothing, however, unless you fund it after setting it up. You can pay a lawyer several thousand dollars to get the legal lingo just right and all your provisions in place, but that alone doesn't mean anything. A wealthy couple recently came to us with unfunded trusts that were exposing them to hundreds of thousands of dollars in estate taxes. We arranged for both to fully fund their trusts with all eligible assets so that they could take better advantage of the federal exemption. An unfunded trust is no trust at all. You must take the essential step of transferring assets and property into it. That is how you put the document to work to protect your assets and keep them out of probate court. Once you establish a functioning trust, you also set up what is called a "pour-over will" to ensure that any of your remaining assets transfer automatically to the trust upon your death.

Trusts come in many varieties. They include revocable and irrevocable, living and testamentary, special needs, charitable, generation-skipping, spendthrift, asset protection, and more. Some have puzzling acronyms such as QTIP, QRPT, or GRAT, but each is designed for a specific important purpose. For now, don't get bogged down in what might seem like a dizzying array of choices. Just know that there are different ways to protect the people in your life. Your advisor can help you determine which type of trust would serve you best. You need only explain what you hope to accomplish, and for whom, and why. And don't think that trusts are only for the ultra-wealthy. Even if you are of more modest means, a trust can eliminate the need for the courts, judges, and last-minute lawyers who would be required if you pass away with assets in your name.

A Will Isn't the Only Way

Though the will is a central document in estate planning, its power is limited. As we have seen, your will has no bearing until you are dead. It doesn't keep your assets out of probate court, where the delays can be frustrating and the expenses significant. It can parcel out your resources to your heirs as you direct, but only in lump sums.

And despite what you put in your will about who will get what, the document does not always come first. Those provisions can be superseded by other agreements. The power of a trust is a prime example. Whatever you place in a trust generally will not be subject to probate and the wording of a will.

Likewise, the beneficiary designation on a 401(k) plan or life insurance policy will get priority over anything that is declared in a will. The assets pass to that beneficiary directly without going through probate. The same is true for payable on death financial accounts and transfer on death real estate deeds. Those contracts will be honored first before the will comes into play. That's why effective estate planning must include regular reviews of those beneficiaries. People sometimes die without having updated the beneficiaries in many years, and the money goes to unintended recipients—such as an ex-spouse.

Charity or Family?

It's a common comment in estate planning whenever the topic of charitable giving comes up: *I'd like to do more giving, but I don't want to deprive my family of their inheritance.* They see their legacy primarily as what they leave for their children and grandchildren. Meanwhile, they are giving a lot of money to the government, which spends their tax money to support whatever it decides is best. Given a choice, most people would rather decide for themselves. Here's what they should know: They could have that choice. With effective planning, using the power of trusts and insurance, families can do more giving without taking away from the inheritance. As less money goes to taxes, more goes to loved ones as well as to cherished institutions and worthy causes.

If you like that idea, talk about it with your family and other heirs. They don't need to agree with your choice of charities, but they should understand your intentions and see that you aren't out to deprive them of their inheritance. Then take a close look at your assets to determine which ones should be assigned to which purposes. It makes sense to give fully taxable assets to charity, since the charity is exempt from taxes on what it gets, and you get a deduction for what you give. Money from your tax-deferred IRA, for example, could be a good charitable choice. If instead you left that money to your kids, they would be obligated to pay all the deferred tax, and the distribution potentially would push them into the highest tax bracket.

On the other hand, the payout from a life insurance policy could be a good resource to leave to your kids, since the money goes to them free of income taxes. They also can claim a step-up in basis on certain assets that they could receive based on its current value rather than on the amount that you originally paid. If your children, for example, inherit stocks from you, they generally would not be taxed on your gains.

Another way to leave money to charity is through your beneficiary listings. You can split the money up by percentages—a third to each of your two children, for example, and the remaining third to your charity of choice. The IRS also allows you to give up to $100,000 annually to eligible charities if you have reached the age when you must begin withdrawing from your tax-deferred retirement plan. The amount given to charity counts toward your required minimum distribution, but you don't pay income tax on it. That's an option only if you don't need the money yourself, of course. Instead, you can benefit a worthy cause, save on taxes, and reduce the extent of your estate.[46]

An interesting trust to consider is the CRT, or charitable remainder trust. It's a good choice if you have assets with a lot of appreciation and would face a steep capital gains tax if you were to sell them. With a CRT, you can donate assets but keep control of them and gain an income from them, for as long as you live—and you get a tax deduction up front for your contribution. Then, upon your death, the charity gets what remains, exempt from taxes. You might also spend some of your interest income to pay the premium on a life insurance policy payable to your heirs after you and your spouse die. That way they could get a tax-free death benefit equivalent to the amount you donated to charity through the CRT. Another option is to set up a charitable lead trust, or CLT. With a CLT, the charity receives the interest from the asset for a set period, after which your heirs get the balance.

Some families also set up a donor-advised fund for their chari-table giving. The family gets a tax deduction for the amount that it contributes every year as a donation to qualified charities, but the money does not go immediately to those charities. Instead, the donations remain in the fund as the family manages the money over time. Eventually it all must go to charities, but the family gains flexibility in deciding which ones will get a donation and when it will happen. Family members can get together annually, perhaps at Thanksgiving, and decide which charities, if any, they will support in the coming year. They need to file only one form for the distribution rather than separate ones, and they get a convenient record of their giving through the years.

---

46   Internal Revenue Service, "Publication 590-B (2020), Distributions from Individual Retirement Arrangements (IRAs)," accessed September 6, 2021, www.irs.gov/publications/p590b.

It's No Secret

In many families, the money is made and lost in three generations. Cultures around the world have recognized that phenomenon. It's known as "shirtsleeves to shirtsleeves," or "clogs to clogs," or "rice paddy to rice paddy." The first generation works hard to create the wealth, rising from the hard labor of the factories or fields. The next generation takes the wealth for granted and squanders it. The children never got their hands dirty or learned much about business and money management. As the family loses its grip on the wealth, the third generation must roll up their shirtsleeves and return to a life of labor, just to get by. The family is back to where it started.

Those who have gained much have much to lose, too, and yet some families don't avail themselves of the tools that could prevent such a consequence. One of those tools is simply good communication of intentions, plans, and values. It should be no secret what you hope to accomplish, and yet those conversations sometimes simply do not happen. Parents don't tell their children about their values or their expectations. Instead of dreaming and planning together, spouses stare into their screens or sit in sullen silence. Even wealthy people sometimes do no estate planning at all.

Find an advisor who will have your back, and let the conversation flow to let them know how best to serve you. Talk freely about what you want to do and why. Let your advisor guide you to the right places where your dreams can take shape and you can accomplish what you wish. You don't need to show up with a bullet list. You don't need to fill out some questionnaire. Instead, begin talking about the people in your family and what they mean to you. What role do they play in the family? What makes them happy, and what are their challenges? How do they get along? Consider what you might do for them both now and after your passing—or a generation after your passing.

This will be your legacy, and you should define what it will look like. If you dive right into the details, that big

Estate planning rises to a higher level when all concerned get together to compare notes and share expectations.

picture can be harder to see. When you focus first on your family vision, you are letting your advisor know which financial tools will be needed to build that vision. Those solutions don't materialize out of thin air. It takes talk to get things done.

Family meetings help immensely. Estate planning rises to a higher level when all concerned get together to compare notes and share expectations. For married couples, the conversation should start between the spouses. Both should be fully aware of the family finances and the estate provisions, although, often, just one spouse takes on that duty while the other remains vague. It helps to do an inventory of all assets, accounts, and properties and how they are titled. That will save your heirs a ton of trouble someday as they try to take the final steps with your estate.

To get the most out of family meetings, prepare an agenda and schedule them, at least annually. You can tell your family that they can come to you anytime with questions, but people are reluctant to talk about money and mortality. Family members likely have real questions and concerns but may worry they would seem like money grubbers if they came to you.

Before the first meeting, set an agenda and encourage your family to ask questions and let you know in advance about any grievances that could stir emotions during the meeting. The agenda should include your specific topics (such as the roles of executor, trustee, and powers of attorney) as well as whatever the others wish to add. Make it formal. Distribute the agenda before the meeting. Keep the minutes of what you discuss and any action steps that family members will take. Be sure that those tasks are distributed fairly. This is not a time for the stream of consciousness that helped when you brainstormed with your advisor. This is a time for information, insights, and clarity.

Share your vision with your family. Get into the details as much as you feel is appropriate, but don't leave anyone in the dark. Yes, some people are inclined to play their cards close to the vest. They don't want their beneficiaries to know the amount of an inheritance, for example. Fine. Talk in percentages then, or generalities—but talk. Let your family know who your trusted advisors are. Explain that they are the ones to contact if necessary.

Make sure that key people, such as your executor and trustee, know their roles and what they are expected to do, and ensure that you understand those roles yourself. Sometimes people just pick someone—often, their spouse—because the lawyer told them that they needed to do it. They might inform the person they chose that the responsibility will be theirs, but the conversation ends there. These are serious legal obligations. An executor must initiate the proceedings to settle the estate, including filing final tax returns. A trustee is the legal owner of a trust's assets and must manage and distribute them as specified. That's a job requiring solid financial understanding. These duties need to be assigned to people with the time and inclination to perform them effectively. Otherwise, they may need to step down and let someone else assume the role.[47]

---

47   Fidelity, "Executor and Trustee Guidelines—Inheritance," accessed September 6, 2021, www.fidelity.com/life-events/inheritance/executor-trustee.

If you have a business, make sure you have an understanding with any partners on operations, finances, and any succession or exit plans. Develop an emergency operations plan in case you die or become incapacitated. By working things out in advance, you can prevent a nightmare if something happens to you.

Good communication also includes providing emergency access to what we call your "digital assets"—that is, your online accounts for which you need usernames and passwords. True, you need to keep them secure from anyone who might misuse them, but you nonetheless should arrange for someone to readily gain access if you become incapacitated, or worse.

You probably have a few dozen passwords. Do you remember them all? If they are stored only in Grandpa's head, the time will come when you won't be able to wake him up to get what you need. Take steps now to ensure that your loved ones won't be locked out and scrambling to attend to details in their time of grief. Does your spouse know how to get into your brokerage account or view your listed beneficiaries? Someone needs to be able to stop the insurance company from making automatic payments on the policy after you die.

On some online password management programs, you can grant emergency access upon request to someone whom you would trust to make decisions on your behalf. The program can keep your usernames and passwords digitally secure, in one place, without the serious security risk you would run if you wrote them down on a tablet tucked in a drawer or on a scrap of paper taped to your computer. You do need to keep that information secure, but that doesn't mean keeping it so top secret that you take it to the grave with you.

Get organized and get ready. Most folks have regretted the time wasted tracking down a document, whether a digital or a paper one, that somehow got slipped into the wrong folder. It happens, and that's why we suggest that our clients email their key documents, such as their trust papers, to themselves. That makes them easy to find by running a quick search of your inbox, even while sitting in a hospital waiting room.

> In essence, estate planning is about how you want to be remembered.

Estate planning is no great mystery, despite the legalese inside all those documents and the fancy terms. In essence, estate planning is about how you want to be remembered. You are taking the loving step of deciding how your life's work will best be used in the world. You are leaving a legacy not only of money, which supports and protects and opens opportunities, but also of the values and traditions that you are confident will continue to serve your family and posterity well. Estate planning is an exercise in caring.

CHAPTER 9

PROTECTION AND PROSPERITY

———————◦◦◦◦◦———————

LET ME SHARE a sad story of a couple who married on Valentine's Day and headed off to Las Vegas, setting aside a thousand dollars as their gambling limit. By the third day of their honeymoon, they had lost all but five dollars. That night the husband dreamed he kept hitting the jackpot and awoke to see that final five-dollar chip on the dresser. Thinking the dream must be a sign, he threw on a bathrobe and rushed back to the casino.

At the roulette table, the groom put his chip on lucky number fourteen, and he won $175 on the 35:1 odds. He let his winnings ride, and again the ball landed on lucky number fourteen, bringing him $6,125. It happened again and again, but when the ecstatic groom was about to wager $7.5 million, the floor manager informed him the casino couldn't pay out if he were to win again. Still in his bathrobe, the young man hailed a taxi to another casino where he again bet every cent on number fourteen—but the ball landed on number fifteen, and he lost it all.

DON'T RUN OUT OF MONEY IN RETIREMENT

Returning to his hotel room, the young man stared dejectedly into the dresser mirror at the drawn lines of a face that had been ecstatic just an hour earlier. "Where were you?" his bride asked.

"Playing roulette."

"Oh. How did you do?"

Turning to face her, he put on a smile. "Not bad, honey," he replied. "I lost five dollars."

The young man in this apocryphal tale had a lot to learn about protecting his gains. There's a lesson here for investors, who likewise stand to lose a bundle if they gamble with their life's savings. When you have made some gains, don't think you are playing with the house's money. It's your money, so be sure to bring good sense to the table.

Jonathan Clements, financial author and longtime columnist for the *Wall Street Journal*, put it this way: "If you want to see the greatest threat to your financial future, go home and take a look in the mirror."

"We Have Met the Enemy ..."

There's a classic line from the old-time comic strip *Pogo*, featuring the creatures of the Okefenokee Swamp in backwoods Georgia. "We have met the enemy," says the philosophizing possum Pogo, "and he is us."

> Investing wisely isn't just about gaining more. It's also about holding on to what you have gained.

This chapter is about how to protect your retirement investments from whatever might take them from you—including you. Investing wisely isn't just about gaining more. It's also about holding on to what you have gained. Both, however, matter. We will examine here how to both protect and enhance your investments so that you will be set for life. We will look at both the defense and the offense.

I don't intend to bore you with too many explicit details about building your portfolio by investing how much, in which assets, at what rate, for how long. You can figure out the numbers with a calculator, and whether an investment is a good one depends on too many factors to list here. But it is always wise, whether you are new to investing or well versed in it, to recognize not only your opportunities but also the dangers you face.

I have a couple of day jobs. One is running my firm, which includes making investment selections. I also work with business owners to grow the value of their companies for maximum sales price. Recently an entrepreneur asked me how he could start with the end in mind to better build his fledgling businesses. My advice was similar to what I tell the owners of more mature companies looking to sell in a few years. We play defense before offense. We start by protecting the existing value and then we work on developing strengths.

That's the approach we will take here as we talk about investments. Don't expect some list of the ten best stocks to buy today and get rich quick. Instead, we will focus first on protection—and the most basic defense isn't to protect against a bear market, or an interest rate spike, or a high tax bracket. It's not fending off a bitter ex-spouse or some opportunist who slips on your sidewalk. Those type of protections must not be overlooked, of course, but investors' most basic defense is to resist the emotional urge to buy high and sell low.

Through the years, I have seen the damage that investors sometimes do to themselves. They make decisions based on attitudes, beliefs, and biases that influence their judgment and can put them at risk. Were it just me pointing this out, you might shrug it off as hypothesis, but researchers at respected universities have concluded likewise. In fact, the field of behavioral economics has produced Nobel laureates, including Daniel Kahneman and Richard Thaler.

I will keep the analytics and footnotes to a minimum here. What I want to impart are not the details of the science but rather the lessons to be learned based on the science—and those lessons often require letting go of one's own take on the truth. "It ain't what a man don't know that makes him a fool," said nineteenth-century humorist Josh Billings, "but what he does know that ain't so."

Specious Beliefs

We each must be aware of our limitations. Investors frequently suffer from what behavioral scientists refer to as "retroactive prescience." That's when we remember only our good decisions and conveniently forget or discount the bad ones.

Much of the value added by a financial advisor results from helping investors avoid mistakes, such as selling low and buying high. A Vanguard report says that such behavioral coaching saves investors 1.5 percent of their portfolio per year.[48]

Some of that protection results from turning to more conservative securities when the stock market looks as if it will be moving south. But some of it also comes from not selling low just as the market is about to bounce back. According to the Dalbar financial research firm, which has been tracking the trends for decades, "One major reason that investor returns are considerably lower than index returns has been the fact that many investors withdraw their invest-

---

48 Vanguard, "The Added Value of Financial Advisors," 2014, http://static.twentyoverten. com/the-added-value-of-financial-advisors.1465329922518.pdf.

ments during periods of market crises. Since 1984, approximately 70 percent of this underperformance occurred during only ten key periods. All these massive withdrawals took place after a severe market decline."[49]

The world of investing attracts a lot of do-it-yourselfers. The DIYers are the ones most vulnerable to the pressures of market volatility. They buy and sell at the wrong times, yet they tend to think they are astute enough to avoid the mistakes that others make. Sometimes they are. Often they aren't.

Let's look at some of the common distortions of judgment that can keep portfolios from performing to their potential.

"I'M BETTER THAN AVERAGE."

"People exaggerate their own skills," says Thaler, who offers the example that if you ask people to rate how well they get along with others, 90 percent will rate themselves above average, which of course is statistically impossible. Likewise, he says, 90 percent of investors think they are above average at picking money managers. "They are optimistic about their prospects and overconfident about their guesses."

Strong confidence is a healthy attribute. When we feel secure in our abilities, we develop a positive framework for getting through life's tough times. However, overconfidence in our investment skills can get us in trouble.

Mutual funds are one example of how we can be our own worst enemies when it comes time to preserve our capital. I'm not picking on mutual funds. I mention them because their active professional management has provided a lot of measurable data. Most mutual

---

49   Dalbar, "Hypothetical Outcomes of Crisis Periods," November 4, 2019, www.dalbar. com/portals/dalbar/cache/docs/Hypothetical%20Outcomes%20of%20Crisis%20 Periods%20v3.pdf.

fund investors expect their investments to consistently outperform the stock market. Statistics show otherwise. About 88 percent of actively managed funds failed to beat their benchmark over a fifteen-year period, according to a 2020 analysis of the SPIVA scorecard (the S&P Indices vs. Active report).[50] The managers who did beat the market did so with no real consistency. It was random. If investment professionals with large supporting teams cannot beat the market, is it rational to think that doing so as a hobby in retirement will lead to better results?

Still, that slim possibility of beating the market keeps hope alive, and that hope breeds overconfidence. Overconfidence leads investors to believe that they will be one of the few who succeed. It turns out that people who trade the most, presumably due to misplaced confidence, produce the lowest returns.[51] That's a phenomenon that studies have borne out. I do have my favorite indicators to tell me when to sell and when to buy. But I know not to be overly confident in interpreting data, so I'll look at a dozen indicators.

The lesson: Be cautious with investment decisions. Look in the mirror and ask yourself why you should feel so confident about risking your money. Why do I say "risking" instead of "investing"? Because the more confident you feel about an investment decision—or about anything, really—the less you are likely to take protective steps. And that, by definition, puts you at higher risk.

50   Eric Rosenberg, "Investment Pros Can't Beat the Stock Market, and It's Not Worth Trying," Business Insider, July 31, 2020, www.businessinsider.com/personal-finance/investment-pros-cant-beat-the-stock-market-2020-7.

51   Brad M. Barber and Terrance Odean, "Trading Is Hazardous to Your Wealth: The Common Stock Investment Performance of Individual Investors," The Journal of Finance 55, no. 2 (April 2020): 773–806, https://faculty.haas.berkeley.edu/odean/Papers%20current%20versions/Individual_Investor_Performance_Final.pdf.

"YESTERDAY'S WINNER IS TODAY'S WINNER."

The academics call it "recency bias" or the "hot hand fallacy." I call it "forecasting for dummies," which is a phrase a speaker used at an investment conference when I was about twenty-five years old. It's the tendency to give too much weight to recent experience while ignoring historical evidence. Investors tend to buy securities that have done well recently—and they do so at their peril. They behave like the gambler who is certain the roulette ball will land on red just because it has done so five times in a row. The market crashes and they don't want to play anymore. The market rallies and they crowd around the table. That's what leads people to buy high and sell low rather than taking advantage of natural market cycles.

The data analytics firm Morningstar, which tracks mutual funds, did a study comparing funds that had the most inflows with those that had the least inflows. Think of them as loved funds versus hated funds. Loved funds were those that investors bought the most of, and hated funds were those that investors sold most heavily. Investors loved the ones that recently had good returns, and they hated the ones that recently had weak returns. In other words, they bought winners and sold losers. However, the three most hated categories of funds had beat the average fund 75 percent of the time and had beat the most loved funds 90 percent of the time.[52]

Recency bias leads investors to buy yesterday's returns, thinking they will endure. They buy the investments that feel good. My dad once told me that "the best trade is usually the one that feels the worst." Or "buy when there's blood in the streets, even if the blood is your own," in the words of Baron Rothschild, the nineteenth-century banker from the wealthy Rothschild family. It's comfortable to

---

52   Ryan Vlastelica, "In One Chart, Here's Why You Should Buy the 'Unloved' Parts of the Equity Market," MarketWatch, January 19, 2018, www.marketwatch.com/story/in-one-chart-heres-why-you-should-buy-the-unloved-parts-of-the-equity-market-2018-01-18.

put winners in your portfolio, but as Warren Buffett warned, "You pay a very high price for a cheery consensus."

FOMO: FEAR OF MISSING OUT

"Men think in herds," the Scottish author Charles Mackay wrote in his 1841 book *Extraordinary Popular Delusions and the Madness of Crowds*. "They go mad in herds, while they only recover their senses slowly, and one by one."[53]

Today, the popular way to describe the herd mentality is FOMO, or fear of missing out. It can be summed up in one word: mania.

In the world of investments, returns are alluring. The trends of the moment are seductive, and perfectly rational people go with the crowd without realizing how they are being influenced. They want to get in on what everyone else seems to be doing. They want to be part of the scene, and so they invest where the crowd is investing. And the crowd is sending up cheers for all their successes. They are silent about their losses. As a result, more and more people pile on to the bandwagon.

Bitcoin is a recent example. A couple years ago, my phone was blowing up with texts from friends, not even clients, wondering whether they should buy Bitcoin. I even did an hour on the radio about it. People had no idea what Bitcoin was, but they were itching to get in on it just because the price was going higher. A decade before, the crowd favored commodities.

If a particular mania lasts long enough, even very conservative investors may abandon long-held beliefs, concerned that they have missed out on what the crowd considers easy money. They forget the basic principles of risk and reward and the value of diversification.

---

53 Charles Mackay, *Extraordinary Popular Delusions and the Madness of Crowds* (Hampshire, UK: Harriman House, 1841).

These manias happen because of the loop of positive feedback. The price goes up just because it is going up. That entices even more people into the mania, with devastating consequences. When speculators get in on the game, prices can soar unrealistically. In an early example, Dutch investors in the 1630s became enthralled with certain tulip varieties. Before the bubble burst, a single bulb at times sold for an amount that was several times a skilled craftsman's annual salary.

The lesson here is to take emotions out of your choices. Don't buy something just because the price is going up. A lot of fools may make a lot of money buying into manias, but you don't want to be that last fool.

I can't think of anywhere besides the stock market where people will buy more of something when the price goes up. If the price of beef goes up, they buy more chicken. If gas prices go up, they drive less. But when stock prices go up, people want more.

More words of wisdom from Warren Buffett: "Be fearful when others are greedy, and greedy when others are fearful." That's not the way investors tend to behave, however. It would seem the human brain isn't wired for the ways of the stock market. It takes discipline to make the right decisions.

"I'M BRILLIANT IF I WIN, UNLUCKY IF I LOSE."

In my college days, I had a buddy named Joe who liked to bet on sports—and he was on a winning streak, placing higher and higher wagers. Joe figured he had the secret to success. He subscribed to a letter issued by someone who seemed to make all the right calls. Until he didn't. One day, Joe lost big-time.

I hadn't thought about Joe until several years later, when I was studying to become a financial advisor and learned about an unethical practice forbidden by the Securities and Exchange Commission. Let's say that, as an advisor, you send out a letter to ten thousand people recommending an investment, but not the same for each. You follow up with a new letter that recommends other investments, but you send it only to those who got the good calls in your first letter. You ignore those who got the bad ones. If you do that over and over, you will end up with a short list of people who see you as an investment genius who always gets it right. Then you ask them for money if they want to hear your next idea. It might seem clever, but it's crooked.

And then it dawned on me: That's what had happened to Joe. My buddy had come to believe that the advice in the letter was brilliant and that he was acting wisely by adhering to it, but he was just getting scammed. He was the victim not only of the scammer but also of himself and his own erroneous beliefs. Some call it the "hot hand fallacy," which is the belief that a person, or an action, is hot or cold depending on past performance. But the hand that you are dealt, or the way your dice roll, or the bet that you place has nothing to do with the previous outcomes—at least not in an honest game.

A hot streak isn't necessarily a scam, of course. Sometimes it's simply luck, nothing nefarious. Fund managers get lucky, too, and a common error among investors is to flock to the ones who have beat their benchmark for a few years in a row. The investors might think they have found a guru, but the outperformance more likely results from something random.

Let's say a fund manager has a fifty-fifty chance of beating the benchmark. That's generous, since statistics show that only about 20 percent of active managers beat their benchmark in any given year. But if a manager can do as well as the flip of a coin, you would expect about a 12 percent probability of coming out ahead three years in a row. With thousands of managers out there, it's likely that many will be able to boast that track record. It's random, though. It's not predictive.

The lesson here is the one that investors often see in legal disclosures: Past performance is not a guarantee of future success. To that, I would add this: Your future success depends on a lot more than your investment returns. Financial planning considers much more.

"ALL THE NEWS THAT FITS MY VIEW."

It's not unusual that a doctoral candidate, in conducting research for a dissertation, will ignore evidence that challenges the hypothesis. We all tend to do this. We favor information that backs up what we already believe. We look for whatever supports our opinions, and we reject whatever casts doubt on them. This aspect of human nature is known as "confirmation bias."

It's hard to find unbiased news sources these days, for example. Fox News attracts viewers who are political conservatives, and MSNBC attracts the political liberals. Instead of offering objective reporting, the channels cater to their viewers' belief systems—and, true, that is my opinion, and I should be open to hearing about any evidence to the contrary. Are you?

My point is that investors, too, tend to seek out the "experts" who will tell them what they want to hear, which is what they already believe. The danger is that they will filter out information that potentially could be useful to them.

Smart investors want to know about anything that might indicate that they could be wrong. With so much at stake, they seek out opposing views that challenge their hypothesis. Instead of just agreeing with themselves, they welcome the opportunity to defend their choices.

FAVORING THE FAMILIAR

Because of my profession, for years people asked me how I felt about their decision to invest in General Electric, which for generations operated a manufacturing plant in our community. If they called it "*the* GE," I knew they had grown up in these parts. Whether or not they knew much about how the company earned money, they felt safe investing in it because the name was so familiar to them. As a known entity, the company felt to them like a solid bet. They didn't really want my insights. They were looking for me to validate their decision.

The old saying that familiarity breeds contempt doesn't hold true for investment decisions. Instead, it breeds comfort. Consider what happened after AT&T was broken into seven regional "Baby Bells" in 1984. The separate stocks were distributed evenly among the shareholders. Within a year, though, those investors had acquired a greater proportion of shares in whichever Bell served the region in which they lived. They perceived more safety in familiarity.

There are many such examples. In Atlanta, people own a lot of Coca-Cola stock. In St. Louis, they're big on Anheuser-Busch. A company's employees often hold an uncomfortably large proportion of their employer's stock in their portfolios. Business owners often choose to open a satellite office in a familiar location instead of where the demographics might better support growth.

On a larger scale, consider that US investors tend to stay with the domestic stocks that are familiar to them. They do so even though the United States accounts for only about a quarter of the global gross domestic product. Many US companies generate much of their profits overseas. In a global economy, it can be shortsighted to exclude international markets as too risky. The diversification, in fact, could significantly strengthen portfolios if the domestic economy faltered.

Nonetheless, US investors tend to take a global view only after foreign stocks have had a boom year—and then they follow the crowd.

The lesson here is don't buy a stock just because you like the name, or have used its products, or admire its mission. It's all right if that's what puts it on your radar screen, but do your homework and examine the cons as well as the pros. Why do you believe that you are making a sound decision? During our office investment meetings, we play devil's advocate with each of our investment selections. We tear them apart and look for all the reasons that we shouldn't be holding them. If we can't defend them, we're just hoping—and hope isn't a strategy.

I suggest that you spend at least as much time researching a major investment as you would put into buying a car or planning a vacation—because if you don't, you might not be buying many more cars or taking many more vacations.

Playing the Offense

Protecting your money clearly requires steps beyond simply recognizing the human foibles that can lead to failure. *That's all very interesting,* people think, *but that's not me.* Instead of looking only at the dangers within, they want to know more about the outside forces that can endanger their portfolios.

We have been focusing so far on what you shouldn't do. Let's play the offense now and look at more things you should do. Earlier we examined the need to plan for medical expenses and other contingencies. And in chapter 6, we explored effective ways to mitigate taxes. Now let's take a closer look at strategies for wise investing.

At Berkshire Money Management, we believe there is a better way than the traditional recommendation that your investment mix should be based on your age. You may have heard the formula, for example, that "100 minus your age equals the proportion of equities you should own." We also gravitate away from traditional theories of long-term investing ("the stock market will always come back") and diversification ("own a little bit of everything, but not too much").

While the investor's age is an important factor in choosing investments, it is not the main factor. The marketplace better defines what is or what is not risky. For example, some might think that owning a short-term Treasury bond fund is "safe" or "conservative"—that is, until the Federal Reserve raises rates and the fund loses money. At BMM, we accept the premise of long-term investing but believe that we add value to your portfolio by identifying potential market crashes and by making the necessary adjustments. And while diversification is of key importance, it shouldn't be an investment mantra, as I will explain in the next section.

I am generally a passive investor. It can make a lot of sense to just buy a security and hold on to it rather than trying to outsmart the market and time its movements in hope of momentary gains. Now and then, though, I will sell securities and try to time the market defensively. It's not so much "let's make a quick buck here." It's more like "let's slow down here."

It generally is better in the long run to reduce volatility by pacing yourself rather than racing for a chance to outpace the market. When I am right about the need to play defense, I have protected your assets. If I am wrong—well, you might have made more money, but you can think of that as the cost of protection. It's like portfolio insurance. You can even choose investments that can protect against the downside while also offering the upside, within limits. In other words, they buffer the volatility, which increases the chances for investment success.

It's all part of the strategy of maintaining the base, of securing the foundation, because without it, how can you expect to build?

I also have my own take on diversification of assets. It certainly is an important means of protecting a portfolio, but doing it right is not as simple as owning a bunch of different stuff. Diversification is not always a sufficient or practical tactic to protect wealth while also promoting growth.

Diversification, put simply, means investing in a variety of financial instruments: large caps and small caps, US stocks and foreign stocks, and don't forget bonds. The idea is to own things that would react differently to the same event. For example, if stocks took a beating in a recession, bonds might act to protect the value of your portfolio.

The intent is to reduce the amount of risk you have but also help maximize returns for a long-term investor with a buy-and-hold strategy. And the math works. If you are investing in emerging-market stocks and they go down by 40 percent, you might say you have a risky portfolio. However, if only 10 percent of your portfolio is allocated to those stocks, then it's not a 40 percent drag on your portfolio—it's a 4 percent drag on your portfolio.

If every piece of your portfolio is working really well at the moment, then it is likely that you are either lucky or not diversified. Probably the latter. I don't know who first said it, but it's true: Diversification means always having to say you're sorry. At any given time, something in a diversified portfolio is bound to be disappointing.

However, I don't like strict adherence to a vigorously diversified portfolio. That

> Wise investors diversify, but they still keep a close watch, and they don't stop thinking.

can lead to trouble, too. Considering that my responsibility is to protect your money, why would I want to stay invested in a security that looks as if it will be going nowhere for a long time—or that seems ready for a downfall?

Wise investors diversify, but they still keep a close watch, and they don't stop thinking. Once upon a time, my company held a lot of international stocks in Europe and Asia. Later, we held very little foreign stocks except through domestic multinationals. That's because international stocks had lagged for a long time. So, while I do preach diversification, I also warn not to diversify for its own sake. There are times to stay away from certain securities for fundamental reasons, and that helps protect the portfolio.

It's increasingly difficult to find a solo practitioner with expertise in investments, Medicare, tax planning, college funding, and so many other areas where people want good guidance. A team practice at a firm that brings together specialists in those areas can better guard your nest egg.

I once approached a seasoned financial advisor, a solo practitioner, about buying his business, but he didn't really seem all that ready to sell. "I just want to stay in the game," he told me, but I sensed that he really wanted to get out of the game. He had a wealth of knowledge on many aspects of financial planning, but he was a one-man show and felt torn about how to best transition his loyal clients. Where else would they get what he was giving them? Well past retirement age, he felt stuck.

My point is that in these days in which retirement planning has become ever more complex, a team approach makes a lot of sense, and the investments and other decisions are best coordinated when those advisors work closely together for efficiency and consistency of strategy.

A Balanced Perspective

"I want to withdraw $9,000 from my account," the elderly client, Gerald, insisted. He seemed exasperated. And he was clear that he meant right away, not tomorrow. Our advisor Scott took the call, and he was understandably skeptical. It was Gerald's money, of course, but why would anyone need that much on the spot?

"So I guess the rainy day for your savings has come," Scott said, fishing for an explanation.

"Never mind. Just get it ready and send it out now."

"I'm just wondering if you'd like to tell me what's up with this," Scott told him.

"Well, I'm worried, because Jeannie—I can't just leave her there, you know? I mean, they said she's in trouble and needs the money now." It made no sense.

"Where's Jeannie?" Scott asked.

"She's in jail!" Gerald blurted out. He went on to explain that someone had contacted him to say his granddaughter had been arrested for something or other—he didn't know what—but for $9,000 bail she could go free right away. "He told me exactly where to take the money, but, see, it has to be cash and then she can be out of that awful place. She's such a good girl. Something's wrong."

Something was wrong all right. Red flags went up all round. "I tell you what," Scott said, "we'll start getting this transaction ready for you, but while we're doing that, have you thought about calling your son to find out what he knows about this?" His son also was a client of ours.

"Well, no, I don't want to do that because the guy—he said he was a lawyer—told me not to let the parents know. I mean, he said it would make matters worse."

"That's all right. You go ahead and call them," Scott said confidently. "You know they care about Jeannie too, right?" He agreed that made sense.

In this case, we had the man's prior authorization to contact his son if we had any questions or concerns. He understood that was an important safeguard. Our industry has implicit rules of confidentiality. Without consent, we cannot identify our clients to anyone. However, older clients often give that consent because they are aware that one day they may need us to contact a family member or someone else they trust. Minutes later, Scott dialed up the parents' home and simply asked whether they had gotten a call.

"Yeah, Dad called. In fact, he's on the other line right now," the son said. "Somebody was trying to scam him, and he was scared to death. But he's okay now, and so is Jeannie, of course. She's not sitting in some jail."

It happens. The crooks out there know full well that older people can be vulnerable to such tactics. In this case, we were able to forestall a potential nightmare, and we did so while keeping Gerald's dignity intact. It was he, after all, who alerted the parents to the scam.

And that's yet one more way in which we can help to protect portfolios. We strive to take an extra level of care and vigilance while serving our clients in a variety of ways for their protection and prosperity.

Financial planners look for the issues that have yet to surface. They try to find the answers to questions still to be asked. They look for the purpose behind the planning, the goals that give meaning to the quest. Sure, our goal is to generate money for our clients, but we also protect their money and help them prepare in many ways for a fulfilling retirement. That's the way to win.

Success has as much to do with attitude as with intellect. Wise investors thoroughly research their selections, and they keep a steady and balanced perspective that remains focused on the goals. They don't go charging after the bull, and they don't cower from the bear, but they pay close attention to both.

I will close this chapter with a few more words of wisdom from the Oracle of Omaha. You likely have heard this before, but it's timeless truth. In the words of Warren Buffett, there are two rules for investing: "Rule number one, never lose money. Rule number two, never forget rule number one."

TO THE FINISH LINE

As THEY APPROACH RETIREMENT, family leaders come to Berkshire Money Management with a variety of concerns, all of which are variations on a theme. Their fundamental question is this: *Are we going to be all right?* And this, fundamentally, is our response: *That depends on what you want to do, so let's start planning for it as soon as possible.* They need clarity on how much they have and how much they will require if they are to meet their goals. They need to know what they should be doing today to get ready.

> In so many ways, retirement planning is a quest for security, which is a primal human need.

In so many ways, retirement planning is a quest for security, which is a primal human need. People feel ill at ease in times of uncertainty. If you already were unsure about your financial prospects, the pandemic likely magnified that angst. It brought new challenges almost daily to families, communities, and nations. It would be nice to think that it brought out the best in everybody—and, yes, there were bright stars in the darkness—but at times it brought out the worst. In anonymity, hiding behind a computer screen, people often find it easier to be rude, even cruel, and to lose perspective.

As social beings, most of us are not wired for solitude. We are designed to draw close and look into one another's eyes. That is what keeps us civil, and that is why the social distancing during the pandemic, though necessary, was so poignantly painful.

A crisis often brings solidarity, for a time, but the afterglow tends to fade as people revert to the grumblings and groanings of daily life. After the 9/11 attacks, we as a nation found a season of unity. It didn't last. And now, as we try again to rebuild, our best hope for a better postpandemic society will be our ability to remember how dreary we felt. Together again, we at least might agree how hard it was to be apart.

Distances divide us. In a world more connected than ever, we must not lose the connections that matter to us most. Sure, video-conferencing is great. It is here to stay and will help people to see eye to eye when they can't truly be eye to eye. Technology in many ways has risen to today's challenges, but I believe most of us would acknowledge that virtual rooms are no substitute for living rooms and conference rooms. At Berkshire Money Management, we embrace technology, but we don't ever want to lose the personal touch with our clients.

Like so many others, you may find yourself approaching retirement, or already there, yet uncertain whether you will be all right. You may be facing some big issue, or standing at a crossroads, and need advice. You have many questions, no doubt. We will do our best to answer those questions as well as the ones you may not yet have thought to ask.

So much has changed in my industry. As a young investment specialist at the turn of the millennium, I wouldn't have thought that my fellow advisors soon would be sporting such monikers as Certified Elder Planning Specialist, or Certified Senior Advisor, or Chartered Retirement Planning Counselor. For that matter, I didn't anticipate that today I would be devoting much of my time to consulting with business owners to help them build their way to greater value and profits.

That is the nature of the variety of services other than investment selection that financial advisors offer today as they add on more and more credentials that demonstrate their dedication to continued education. That shift evolved as investors learned the stark truth that they generally could do as well or better by investing passively in index funds than by committing their money to an investment manager.

> Financial planning isn't just about investing. It's about the array of services that work together to serve you best.

So why consult with an advisor at all? The answer is clear: Maintaining one's financial health involves a lot more than stock picking. Financial planning isn't just about investing. It's about the array of services that work together to serve you best. Fiduciary advisors who are required to put their clients' interests first won't promise returns that will beat the market. Instead, they will work with you diligently to find ways to protect what you have worked a lifetime to accomplish.

An advisor's experience doesn't matter if what you get is a bad experience. Because people tend to think one advisor is as good as the next, they don't often switch to someone else. They stay with the known entity, which means, sadly, that an advisor who has been around a long time might also be an advisor who has done a terrible job for a long time. Talent always trumps experience. I'm not worthy because of my three decades of experience. My reputation must be built on how well I serve my clients today.

I love what I do as a business owner and as a member of my community. I live for the high-five moments. Competitive by nature, I relish the entrepreneurial spirit of building something and sharing the excitement. My colleagues would agree, I am sure, that our greatest satisfaction comes from helping people to achieve not only their financial needs but also their dreams. One family at a time, we are strengthening our community. Together, we are advancing to the finish line.

IMPORTANT DISCLOSURES:

1. Registration with the SEC should not be construed as an endorsement or an indicator of investment skill, acumen, or experience.

2. Investments in securities are not insured, protected, or guaranteed and may result in loss of income and/or principal.

3. This book is distributed for informational purposes, and it is not to be construed as an offer, solicitation, recommendation, or endorsement of any particular security, products, or services. Nothing in this book is intended to be or should be construed as individualized investment advice. All content is of a general nature and solely for educational, informational, and illustrative purposes. To learn more about the firm's services please request and review our disclosure documents.

4. Industry registrations, designations, recognitions, or awards should not be construed as an endorsement or a recommendation to retain the Advisor by the granting entity or any regulatory authority. A detailed description of listed professional designations is available upon request in our Firm's Form ADV Part 2B.

5. Nothing in this book is intended to imply and should not be construed to imply that services comparable to those offered by our firm cannot be found elsewhere.

6. This book may include opinions and forward-looking statements. All statements other than statements of historical fact are opinions and/or forward-looking statements (including words such as "believe," "estimate," "anticipate," "may," "will," "should," and "expect"). Although we believe that the beliefs and expectations reflected in such forward-looking statements are reasonable, we can give no assurance that such beliefs and expectations will prove to be correct. Various factors could cause actual results or performance to differ materially from those discussed in such forward-looking statements. All expressions of opinion are subject to change. You are cautioned not to place undue reliance on these forward-looking statements. Any dated information is published as of its date only. Dated and forward-looking statements speak only as of the date on which they are made. We undertake no obligation to update publicly or revise any dated or forward-looking statements.

7. Any references to outside data, opinions, or content are listed for informational purposes only and have not been verified for accuracy by the Advisor. Third-party views, opinions, or forecasts do not necessarily reflect those of the Advisor or its employees.

8. Advisor is not licensed to provide and does not provide legal, tax, or accounting advice to clients. Advice of qualified counsel or accountant should be sought to address any specific situation requiring assistance from such licensed individuals.

9. Some of the persons and/or names in this book may be fictional and intended to either illustrate a concept and/or protect a subject's privacy.

10. Some scenarios and outcomes described in this book may not be typical or easy to replicate in the future and are intended to illustrate a principle or a concept.